Preaching
The Parables

Series III, Cycle C

Dallas A. Brauninger

CSS Publishing Company, Inc.
Lima, Ohio

Copyright © 2003 by
CSS Publishing Company, Inc.
Lima, Ohio

Scripture quotations are from the *New Revised Standard Version of the Bible*, copyright 1989 by the Division of Christian Education of the National Council of the Churches of Christ in the USA. Used by permission.

Library of Congress Cataloging-in-Publication Data

Brauninger, Dallas A., 1943-
  Preaching the parables. Series III, Cycle C / Dallas A. Brauninger.
    p. cm.
Includes bibliographical references and index.
  ISBN 0-7880-1964-3 (pbk. : alk. paper)
  1. Jesus Christ—Parables. 2. Bible. N.T. Gospels—Homiletical use. 3. Lectionary preaching. I. Title.
BT375.3.B73 2003
251'.6—dc21

2003003524

For more information about CSS Publishing Company resources, visit our website at www.csspub.com or e-mail us at custserv@csspub.com or call (800) 241-4056.

ISBN 0-7880-1964-3

To Sam

Table Of Contents

Introduction

What draws us toward belief? Is it that mysterious connecting point somewhere within the movement from mind of God to mind of storyteller to mind of hearer? Jesus told parables to ordinary persons with ordinary quandaries; yet a parable yields a universal truth that transcends time and waits for any reader to discover. As an art form, all that it speaks cannot be set on a page of words. Similarly, searching the heart for full understanding of a parable is an act of faith.

We also come to these parables as ordinary persons with universal dilemmas. No matter who we are, each time we meet the parable, we come as slightly different persons. While the cynic might suppose it depends upon what a parable tells us when it speaks to something within, is that not our receptivity to the Spirit of God speaking?

In uniting past with present, readers explore: What dimension of the soul that needs tending does the parable address? What is the parable's surprise? What moves us into hope? How does its point become obvious? How do its characters relate today to us? What does it tell us about God?

Sparking the questions is germinal to exploring a biblical text. While this book offers a read filled with information for the sermon writer to develop, its content design offers more than the ho-hum. It avoids presenting a ready-made cloak of sermon words. Its goal is to invite.

Series design is sequel to the writer's popular *Preaching The Miracles* (Series II, Cycles A-B-C). The first section of each chapter presents the text of a parable within the lectionary cycle.

Section Two, "What's Happening?" is a synopsis of points of action. By reviewing the action of the parable, readers define its movement, conflict, and change or resolution.

Section Three, "Spadework," lifts up significant words with an open-ended survey of Hebrew and New Testament writings. While it is not the writer's aim to present a scholarly word study, hopefully this study offers more than pabulum. A Word Study Index locates selected words by parable.

Section Four, "Parallel Scripture," compares parallel stories or words/concepts where the parable text is unique.

Section Five, "Chat Room," aims to engage readers in a variety of imaginary electronic exchanges through online chats. This invention invites readers, worship leaders, and listening congregations to become askers of questions. Here participants suspend the usual barriers of time and place. These chats range from an interview with a parable character to friends browsing each other's ideas to a conversation of self with self.

The writer aims here also to avoid the conclusive by offering pondering and insightful dialogue snatches that invite reflection. Beyond study, the conversational visit is appropriate as a dramatic sermon resource or chancel reading.

What speaks? As we become aware of how God speaks through parables, we also hear better our inner voice and understand ourselves anew. We may even find the connecting point that bridges the soul of a parable character with our own.

Parable 1

The Sign Of The Fig Tree

Luke 21:25-36

1. Text

"There will be signs in the sun, the moon, and the stars, and on the earth distress among nations confused by the roaring of the sea and the waves. [26] People will faint from fear and foreboding of what is coming upon the world, for the powers of the heavens will be shaken. [27] Then they will see 'the Son of Man coming in a cloud' with power and great glory. [28] Now when these things begin to take place, stand up and raise your heads, because your redemption is drawing near."

[29] Then he told them a parable: "Look at the fig tree and all the trees; [30] as soon as they sprout leaves you can see for yourselves and know that summer is already near. [31] So also, when you see these things taking place, you know that the kingdom of God is near. [32] Truly I tell you, this generation will not pass away until all things have taken place. [33] Heaven and earth will pass away, but my words will not pass away.

[34] "Be on guard so that your hearts are not weighed down with dissipation and drunkenness and the worries of this life, and that day catch you unexpectedly, [35] like a trap. For it will come upon all who live on the face of the whole earth. [36] Be alert at all times, praying that you may have the strength to escape all these things that will take place, and to stand before the Son of Man."

2. What's Happening?

First Point Of Action

Jesus' preface to this parable appears at first to be disastrous news, then readers discover that the news is good. People will see signs in nature and in the way nations interact. People will react to these changes because of fear and foreboding of what is coming.

Second Point Of Action

Then they will see that what is coming with power and great glory is the Son of Man, coming in a cloud.

Third Point Of Action

Jesus tells them their response: Stand up and raise your heads. Your redemption draws near. This event is worthy of celebration.

Fourth Point Of Action

Jesus tells the parable. Look at what the fig tree and all trees tell you about summer's coming when they begin to sprout leaves.

Fifth Point Of Action

Similarly, observe the dependable signs in human nature that tell you to count on a change to happen.

Sixth Point Of Action

Jesus further reassures with the final aspects of certainty. Jesus' word can be trusted. The world will not change until everything is ready.

Seventh Point Of Action

Jesus defines the proper attitude of preparation. Avoid being caught unexpectedly because of faulty lifestyle and attitude. No one is exempt. Stay alert. A proper defense embraces God by preparing the heart first, that is, praying first for strength to escape all that will take place, and then to stand before "the Son of Man."

3. Spadework

As Soon As

This little phrase carries the weight of the parable. *As soon as* this happens, this will happen. Depend upon it. Trust it to happen. It is part of the design. *As soon as* you observe the leaves sprout on the fig tree, you can trust that summer is already near. The fig requires summer's warmth to return to full life. As clearly, *as soon as* other signs of change begin to show, trust that the realm of God is near. Pay attention and you need not be surprised, but ready.

Fig

As Americans may have named the elm earlier and now the oak or maple as a first thought of common tree, people in Jesus' locality may have thought first of the fig tree. The fig, the olive, and the grapevine, often referred to in scripture, were plentiful specimens for metaphor. Folk also coveted the fig tree for its shade. It signaled that its owner was wealthy. (See Cycle C, Parable 3, The Fruitless Fig Tree.)

Parable

Of the Gospels, Luke refers to "parable" most often with sixteen uses, but he makes no reference to "parables." "Parable(s)" occurs in Matthew fifteen times and a dozen times in Mark, but not at all in John.

Unlike the miracle stories where Jesus is the doer of the deeds, in the parables Jesus is the teller of stories. How the parable makes the meaning clear or obvious is a worthy query to bring to a parable. Also consider if the parable draws a hearer farther into the puzzle of understanding what Jesus has in mind by offering the parable.

While in Hebrew Scripture, one finds the words "parable" or "parables" only in Psalm 78:2-4, this Psalm provides a telling passage. Beginning, "I will open my mouth in a parable," "open" suggests both the action of speaking and the disclosure of revealing what once was hidden or mysterious.

The Psalmist suggests a radical change in that "dark sayings" (v. 2b), still a mystery to the reader if not to the Psalmist, will no longer be hidden from the next generation. The next generation will continue to pass them on.

The term "dark sayings" is as suggestive as the frightening predictions of what is to come in the present parable. However, the simultaneous telling of "the glorious deeds of the Lord, and his might, and the wonders that he has done" (v. 4b) brings to mind the positive outcome foretold in the present parable.

Luke draws us farther into the puzzling and mysterious secrets of the meaning of a parable in Luke 8:9-10. When the disciples ask Jesus the meaning of the parable of the sower, he refers them to the prophecy of Isaiah that his words fulfill.

The disciples are "given to know the secrets of the kingdom of God; but to others I speak in parables, so that 'looking they may not perceive, and listening they may not understand' " (Luke 8:10). (See Isaiah 6:8-12, the "Whom shall I send" and "Here am I; send me" passage.)

Continuing the story of our attempts to comprehend the ways and being of God, the season of Advent introduces a new perspective to the parable of The Sign Of The Fig Tree. Advent prepares us for the birth of a storyteller who conveys the truth in parables that speak with symbols meaningful at the level of the soul.

Signs

From this first Sunday of Advent, the signs of foreshadowing have begun. They are signs of dependability and stability, signs of what we can count on, signs of change, and signs to which we must become alert. Refer to other signs of foreboding in Isaiah 13:10, Joel 2:10, Zephaniah 1:15, and Revelation 6:13.

Son Of Man

Of the sixteen Lukan parables selected for this lectionary cycle, this phrase appears only in this story and in the parable found in the midsummer lection, the parable of The Watching Servants. (See Cycle C, Parable 9.) "Son of Man" appears twice in The Sign Of The Fig Tree. The first instance in Luke 21:27 is part of a phrase set in quotations, "the Son of Man coming in a cloud," referring to Daniel 7:13-14; Matthew 16:27, 26:64; and Luke 9:27, 18:7-8. Luke 21:36 provides the second reference, "to stand before the Son of Man."

Of the 79 instances of the Son of Man in the New Testament, 65 uses occur in the Synoptic Gospels (Matthew - 27 times, Mark - thirteen, Luke - 25) and in John, thirteen. By contrast, of the 34 New Testament references to "the Son of God," fourteen are found in the Synoptic Gospels — six in Matthew, two in Mark, and six in Luke — with eight in John.

When a phrase is used as often as the Son of Man, one begins to look more closely at its emphasis. Perhaps this was of Jesus' design. Jesus was a person, yet he was more than a person. Did he want to awaken this realization in others? Is he also reminding himself of who he is as well as Whose he is? The phrase designates a title. It suggests that Jesus has claimed his calling. Jesus will use this reference to himself until it arouses the curiosity and finally the faithfulness of others.

Jesus differentiates between the Son of Man and the Holy Spirit: "Whoever speaks a word against the Son of Man will be forgiven, but whoever speaks against the Holy Spirit will not be forgiven, either in this age or in the age to come." (See Matthew 12:32.)

Luke grounds Jesus' beginnings in genealogy: "[Jesus] was the son (as was thought) of Joseph son of Heli, ... the son of Enos, the son of Seth, the son of Adam, the son [sic, lower case son] of God" (Luke 3:38). Here the Son of Man is introduced as we first meet Jesus, the vulnerable infant born of a man and a woman, the human connection, the God to the human family bond.

In Jesus' words, the adult Son of Man also is vulnerable. Jesus' references to himself as the Son of Man persist in reminding us of Jesus' human origin. (See especially Luke 9:44, " 'Let these words sink into your ears: The Son of Man is going to be betrayed into human hands.' ")

However, the Son of Man is always in relationship to God the Parent. (See John 8:28, "So Jesus said, 'When you have lifted up the Son of Man, then you will realize that I am he, and that I do nothing on my own, but I speak these things as the Father instructed me.'")

To contrast, in Luke from the tempting devil and the demons Jesus drew out of the ill to the assembly of elders who led him away to the high council, Jesus' adversaries referred to him as the Son of God. (See Luke 4:3, 9, 41; and 22:70.)

The timeless and universal human querying has begun. When the people refer to Jesus, they use the term "the Son of God." (See Luke 22:70, "All of them asked, 'Are you, then, *the Son of God*?' He said to them, '*You* say that I am.'" At his death, the centurion said these words: "Truly this man was God's Son!" (Matthew 27:54b and Mark 15:39). However, in the Lukan telling, the centurion side-steps, "Certainly this man was innocent!" (Luke 23:47b).

The people do not refer to Jesus as "the Son of Man" until in the Gospel ascribed to John. One from the crowds asks him outright, "Who is this Son of Man?" (John 12:34b). "Who is this Son of Man?" was their question. It is also ours.

4. Parallel Scripture

While this nature parable has no Gospel parallel, cross-references given below may offer further insight into its meaning.

The Signs
In the Lukan passage, Jesus speaks of the nature signs — the sun, moon, and stars — and the signs of human distress — confusion, fear, and foreboding. (See Luke 21:25.) Mark's writer tells us what to look for in the nature signs: "[T]he sun will be darkened, and the moon will not give its light, and the stars will be falling from heaven" (Mark 13:24-25a). Here Mark says, "and the powers in the heavens will be shaken" (Mark 13:24b); whereas, Luke prefaces the same words with these: "People will faint from fear and foreboding of what is coming upon the world, for the powers of the heavens will be shaken" (Luke 21:26).

The writer of Matthew warns that we "know how to interpret the appearance of the sky, but you cannot interpret the signs of the times" (Matthew 16:3). Matthew also speaks about signs in nature:

14

"The sun will be darkened, and the moon will not give its light; the stars will fall from heaven, and the powers of heaven will be shaken" (Matthew 24:29).

The Son Of Man

Luke 21:27 reads, "Then they will see 'the Son of Man coming in a cloud' with power and great glory." Mark reads, "in clouds" and "great power and glory" (see Mark 13:26). Mark offers this additional action: "Then he will send out the angels, and gather his elect from the four winds, from the ends of the earth to the ends of heaven" (Mark 13:27). Matthew reads, "Then the sign of the Son of Man will appear in heaven, and then all the tribes of the earth will mourn, and they will see 'the Son of Man coming on the clouds of heaven' with power and great glory" (Matthew 24:30).

The Parable

Luke prefaces the parable with these words: "Then he told them a parable:" (see Luke 21:29a). Mark makes a direct presentation of the fig tree as a metaphor.

In Luke, Jesus instructs us to "look at the fig tree and all the trees" (Luke 21:29b). Mark and Matthew speak only of the fig, "From the fig tree learn its lesson:" (see Mark 13:28 and Matthew 24:32).

Luke says, "as soon as they sprout leaves" (Luke 21:30a), while Mark, for once less cryptic and more poetic, says, "as soon as its branch becomes tender and puts forth its leaves" (Mark 13:28b). The text from Matthew is identical here. (See Matthew 24:32.)

Luke then says, "[Y]ou can see for yourselves and know that summer is already near" (Luke 21:30), while Mark and Matthew say only, "[Y]ou know that summer is near" (Mark 13:29b and Matthew 24:32b).

Luke adds, "So also, when you see these things taking place, you know that the kingdom of God is near" (Luke 21:31). Matthew says, "all these things, you know that he is near, at the very gates" (Matthew 24:33). Mark says, "that he is near" then adds, "at the very gates" (Mark 13:29).

The next two lines: "Truly I tell you, this generation will not pass away until all things have taken place. Heaven and earth will pass away, but my words will not pass away" (Luke 21:32-33), are identical except that Mark and Matthew say, "all these things" (Mark 13:30 and Matthew 24:34-35).

The Warning

The words of warning are quite different between Mark and Luke; however the message is the same. Both say to be on guard. Luke says, "Be on guard" (Luke 21:34) and "Be alert at all times" (Luke 21:36). Mark says, "Beware, keep alert" (Mark 13:33) and "Keep awake" (Mark 13:35). "Keep awake therefore, for you do not know on what day your Lord is coming" (Matthew 24:42).

Mark emphasizes that no one, "neither the angels in heaven, nor the Son, but only the Father" (Mark 13:32) knows the day or hour of the coming. (See also Mark 13:33.) Luke expresses more concern for the person who is to be on guard, saying to be on guard "so that your hearts are not weighed down with dissipation and drunkenness and the worries of this life, and that day catch you unexpectedly, like a trap" (Luke 21:34-35).

Luke says to "be alert at all times, praying that you may have the strength to escape all these things that will take place, and to stand before the Son of Man" (Luke 21:36). In Matthew, "Therefore you also must be ready, for the Son of Man is coming at an unexpected hour" (Matthew 24:44).

The Habakkuk Parallel

Drawing attention to a world that seems in perennial turmoil, this Lukan passage bears a resemblance to the words of the Hebrew prophet Habakkuk (Habakkuk 3:16-19).

The first parallel is the cognizance of change: "There will be signs in the sun, the moon, and the stars, and on the earth distress among nations confused by the roaring of the sea and the waves" (Luke 21:25) and "Though the fig tree does not blossom, and no fruit is on the vines; though the produce of the olive fails, and the fields yield no food; though the flock is cut off from the fold, and there is no herd in the stalls" (Habakkuk 3:17).

Second is the common, visceral response to fear: "People will faint from fear and foreboding of what is coming upon the world, for the powers of the heavens will be shaken" (Luke 21:27) and "I hear, and I tremble within; my lips quiver at the sound. Rottenness enters into my bones, and my steps tremble beneath me" (Habakkuk 3:16a).

Third is the suggested response to the uncertainty of the times coupled with the anticipation of change: "Be alert at all times, praying that you may have the strength to escape all these things that will take place, and to stand before the Son of Man" (Luke 21:36) and "I wait quietly for the day of calamity to come upon the people who attack us" (Habakkuk 3:16b).

The reminder of God's presence of strength through the difficult times and God's redemptive salvation comprise the fourth parallel: Compare, "Then they will see 'the Son of Man coming in a cloud' with power and great glory. Now when these things begin to take place, stand up and raise your heads, because your redemption is drawing near" (Luke 21:27-28) with the affirmation of Habakkuk, "[Y]et I will rejoice in the Lord; I will exult in in the God of my salvation. God, the Lord, is my strength" (Habakkuk 3:18-19).

5. Chat Room

Person From Early Christian Era: I must admit to becoming uneasy yesterday when Jesus began talking to us. There is so much that we cannot control. From my perspective, the whole world is almost always in chaos. We barely get calmed down then something else erupts. I find this unsettling. Now Jesus tells us the things of nature are about to turn tumultuous. I never have been good at reading the signs unless I look back in time. I must tell you that I see little hope.

Person From 2003: This mess continues into our millennium as well, but I do have a different viewpoint. Whenever we are in a time of unrest, whether the commotion is personal or its scope is international or the result of natural disaster, that unease overrides everything we do.

We forget then about the times of relative stability. We seem the most fearful during such times. We forget that it is temporary. We are most vulnerable then to forgetting about the strength of hope.

Early CE: For me, such periods overshadow even the good times. Fear and foreboding are strong forces. I know where I personally have been lacking and wonder if my ways have contributed to the signs I see around me. Maybe such thinking gives me too much power. It could be that the world is out of control despite anything that I have done or that I could do. Maybe it is too late.

Person From Idaho: You overlook the power of the "then." Hello, I'm joining you from Idaho. What always surprises me is Christ's knack for inserting the one little word that changes everything. Here, first he scares us until we quake with apprehension. He gains our attention. We start looking at how we live. When he inserts the "then," it all settles into place. "Then," Christ tells us, "they will see that what is coming with power and great glory is the Son of Man coming in a cloud."

CE: Thanks for the reinforcement, Idaho. We do have reason to choose hope over fear. Jesus' preface to this parable appears at first to be disastrous news. Of course, terror is terror. We have seen plenty of that throughout the ages.

In my day, it also appears to squash the circle of calm. Nevertheless, I believe that God comes out on the side of hope despite the struggle. This is the season of Advent, the waiting season. Into the mess of your ancient world, God brought the hope of an infant named Emmanuel, God-with-us. Into our troubled midst today also, the spirit of God continues to re-emerge. We have to look for hope in the small, day-to-day signs of God's presence in the midst of uncertainty.

Idaho: Check out the whole passage. Christ does not stop with the parable. He offers another response to terror to calm the quaking within. We must meet the presence of our vulnerability and walk through it to get to the other side. Christ shows us the way through. He says, "Stand up and raise your heads because your redemption is drawing near." Hey, this is celebratory. Christ is talking about saving. Saving is about new beginnings. This is hope-talk, people.

CE: It seems to me that these parables Jesus tells us only add to the confusion. At least with the miracles, even if we must make a faith leap, we do witness a concrete change to a real problem. With the parable, I feel that I am the one left to make sense of it.

2003: Indeed, you and I bring to a parable our own situations and our own understanding at a given time. A parable is a story with an unexpected yet strangely predictable ending *because* its author is Christ. Let us give the parables a chance to surprise us. Let us give them a chance to change us. God continues to provide opportunity for the a-ha of understanding. In order to move us into hope, God sometimes sends a miracle. Sometimes, God responds with a parable. Always, God responds.

Fig Tree: Now, don't laugh. I am a fig tree, and I do have a talking precedent. Check out Judges 9:5-15, another albeit less familiar Hebrew story of sibling rivalry. When Jotham's brother Abimelech wanted to become king, he killed all of his siblings except Jotham.

In a metaphorical story, he sent a warning to the lords of Shechem after they made Abimelech king. Anyway, Jotham concealed the warning in a message spoken through an olive tree, a fig tree, and a grape vine.

CE: And what does that story have to do with this parable?

Fig: The other trees approached us, in turn, asking us to give up doing what we were designed by nature to do. In turn, we refused. So they went to the bramble, who represented Abimelech. You can read the outcome for yourself.

My point is, much as I would like to shine with specially coded messages, in the present parable the fig tree is a common tree, part of the dependable natural world. This is a cause and effect parable.

We can trust natural law: lengthening days, warming, and rainfall to awaken the swelling of my buds and the sprouting of my leaves. Cause and effect, I say.

Signs of renewed life and signs of summer interplay as does how the human family treats the earth — poisons, ill-use, waste and the resultant air pollution, resource exhaustion, and climatic changes that are more than cyclical do have an effect upon the natural world.

CE: Then you would counsel us to attend to subtle sky changes, the moisture of the air, the activity or hush of birds, our sudden grouchiness, or our sense of foreboding before the tumult begins to lash at us and we become trapped.

Fig: Both literally and by metaphor. What other truth does your Christ want the fig to convey to you? Ask, today, what signs in human nature you notice that tell you to count on something to happen. Your Christ knows that to ignore these signs will lead to trouble.

Heeding them while you still can leads to turning things around or at the least being able to withstand the calamity. Cause and effect, that is the process. Heeding these signs of inner and outer unrest also can bring an effect, that of remedy. Then your attitude toward changing signs will become that of watchful waiting. Advent still happens in Idaho, I say.

2003: Yet, even when there is destruction, the urge to survive and thrive again endures. That is the reconnecting with God story, the God with us and the God for us story.

Fig: Green is good. So now is the time to read the cause and effect signs of your life. Get ready now in the midwinter. Practice watchful waiting and persistent preparation for our springtime resurrection.

Parable 2

The Blind Leading The Blind

Luke 6:39-49

1. Text

[Jesus] also told them a parable: "Can a blind person guide a blind person? Will not both fall into a pit? [40] A disciple is not above the teacher, but everyone who is fully qualified will be like the teacher. [41] Why do you see the speck in your neighbor's eye, but do not notice the log in your own eye? [42] Or how can you say to your neighbor, 'Friend, let me take out the speck in your eye,' when you yourself do not see the log in your own eye? You hypocrite, first take the log out of your own eye, and then you will see clearly to take the speck out of your neighbor's eye.

[43] "No good tree bears bad fruit, nor again does a bad tree bear good fruit; [44] for each tree is known by its own fruit. Figs are not gathered from thorns, nor are grapes picked from a bramble bush. [45] The good person out of the good treasure of the heart produces good, and the evil person out of evil treasure produces evil; for it is out of the abundance of the heart that the mouth speaks.

[46] "Why do you call me 'Lord, Lord,' and do not do what I tell you? [47] I will show you what someone is like who comes to me, hears my words, and acts on them. [48] That one is like a man building a house, who dug deeply and laid the foundation on rock; when a flood arose, the river burst against that house but

could not shake it, because it had been well built. [49]
But the one who hears and does not act is like a man
who built a house on the ground without a foundation.
When the river burst against it, immediately it fell, and
great was the ruin of that house."

2. What's Happening?

First Point Of Action
Jesus teaches about sight, insight, and sagacity.

Second Point Of Action
Jesus speaks about the source of good versus inferior productivity of fruit trees and of the human heart.

Third Point Of Action
Jesus talks about the base of heeding the teachings of a sound foundation.

3. Spadework

Blind
Images of blindness have ill served those who are blind. Most of the 59 biblical references categorize as impotent those who are blind. They are among those imprisoned by their body in some way and needing rescue. Their vulnerability becomes their identity. (See Jeremiah 31:8 and 2 Samuel 5:6.) John assigned those who are blind as among the invalid. (Note the double meaning.) See John 5:3.

Certain Hebraic rules applied when relating to those who are blind: "You shall not ... put a stumbling block before the blind" (Leviticus 19:14a). "Cursed be anyone who misleads a blind person on the road" (Deuteronomy 27:18).

A law in Leviticus that everyone living with a disability must get beyond before serving God reads: "No one of your offspring throughout their generations who has a blemish may approach to offer the food of his God. For no one who has a blemish shall draw near, one who is *blind* or lame, or ..." (Leviticus 21:16b-20).

22

Despite the scourge of blindness in Jesus' time, hope does come to those with vulnerabilities. God takes action: "The Lord sets the prisoners free; the Lord opens the eyes of the blind." (See Psalm 146:7-9.) To those with weak hands, feeble knees, fearful hearts, closed eyes, and stopped up ears, "he will come and save you. Then the eyes of the blind shall be opened ..." (Isaiah 35:5). (See also Isaiah 29:18 and 42:7.)

Those who know neither justice nor righteousness "grope like the blind along a wall, groping like those who have no eyes; we stumble at noon as in the twilight, among the vigorous as though we were dead" (Isaiah 59:10). What an image, albeit negative. No one, especially those without sight, wants the embarrassment of walking like those who are blind. A mobility cane offers somewhat of an improvement, but a dog guide brings a cadence at times as smooth as that of a seeing person. As part of God's retribution, God "will bring such distress upon people that they shall walk like the blind; because they have sinned against the Lord, their blood shall be poured out like dust, and their flesh like dung" (Zephaniah 1:17). Was this the beginning of associating blindness with having "sinned against the Lord" that Jesus corrected?

Jesus changes current thinking, clarifying in the healing of the man at Jericho that blindness is not the result of sin[1]: "Neither this man nor his parents sinned; he was born blind so that God's works might be revealed in him" (John 9:3). Inviting those who are blind to eat at the banquet table, Jesus acknowledges they exist as valid persons, are worthy of healing, and are welcome at the table. However, they were invited out of charity because in that day they could not repay the invitation. (See Places Of Honor, Luke 14:13-14, Cycle C, Parable 11.)

Jesus understands healing the blind as part of his ministry: "The Spirit of the Lord is upon me, because he has anointed me to bring good news to the poor. He has sent me to proclaim release to the captives and recovery of sight to the *blind,* to let the oppressed go free" (Luke 4:18).

Persons with blindness also must overcome the oppression of several images that have become figures of speech: "[G]rope in the darkness" (Deuteronomy 28:29); "taking a bribe to blind one's eyes

23

to" something (1 Samuel 12:3); "turn a blind eye" (Proverbs 28:27); and "blind to our ways" (Jeremiah 12:4). Scripture defined the metaphor as one without knowledge. (See Isaiah 42:18-20 and 56:10.)

"Bring forth the people who are blind, yet have eyes...!" (Isaiah 43:8). Is this a figure of speech or an invitation for inclusion? Perhaps it is both. Is it an affirmation of other ways to perceive when one does not see?

Matthew refers to "blind" in eleven verses, Mark uses it four times, Luke uses it six times, and John uses it in nine verses. Most mention of physical blindness in the New Testament lies within the context of being healed. See Matthew 9:27, 12:22, 15:30, 20:30, and 21:14; Mark 8:22 and 10:49-52.

Jesus acknowledges this gift of healing when his disciples ask if he is the one "who is to come." "Go and tell John what you hear and see: the blind receive their sight ... And blessed is anyone who takes no offense at me" (Matthew 11:4-6). (See also Luke 7:21.)

In Matthew 15:11-14 as well as the present text, Jesus uses a metaphorical reference to the lack of understanding among religious leaders: "Let them alone; they are blind guides of the blind. And if one blind person guides another, both will fall into a pit."

Again in Matthew 23:16, Jesus criticizes the Pharisees who try to convert others. He uses "blind" five times in this woe:

"Woe to you, *blind guides*, who say, 'Whoever swears by the sanctuary is bound by nothing, but whoever swears by the gold of the sanctuary is bound by the oath' " (Matthew 23:16);

"You *blind fools!* For which is greater, the gold or the sanctuary that has made the gold sacred?" (Matthew 23:17);

"*How blind you are*! For which is greater, the gift or the altar that makes the gift sacred?" (Matthew 23:19);

"You *blind guides*! You strain out a gnat but swallow a camel!" (Matthew 23:24); and

"You *blind Pharisee*! First clean the inside of the cup, so that the outside also may become clean" (Matthew 23:26).

Years later, John interprets the metaphor to the questioning Pharisees: "Jesus said, 'I came into this world for judgment so that those who do not see may see, and those who do see may become blind.' Some of the Pharisees near him heard this and said to him,

24

'Surely we are not blind, are we?' Jesus said to them, 'If you were blind, you would not have sin. But now that you say, "We see," your sin remains' " (John 9:39-41). Also, "He has blinded their eyes and hardened their heart, so that they might not look with their eyes, and understand with their heart and turn — and I would heal them" (John 12:40).

(The) Foundation

Of references to "the foundation," six passages stand out. From the beginning, creation was a deliberate, solid plan that began with the laying of a foundation: "Long ago you laid the foundation of the earth ..." (Psalm 102:25).

All houses and halls that Solomon built began with a strong foundation of huge stones. (See 1 Kings 7:9-10.) No experimenting here, these foundation stones have been tested. "[T]herefore thus says the Lord God, See, I am laying in Zion a foundation stone, a tested stone, a precious cornerstone, a sure foundation: 'One who trusts will not panic' " (Isaiah 28:16). Neither should a foundation be the work of an unknown builder: "Thus I make it my ambition to proclaim the good news, not where Christ has already been named, so that I do not build on someone else's foundation" (Romans 15:20).

By metaphor, consider what intangible substances you choose to incorporate into the foundation of your being: "Righteousness and justice are the foundation of your throne; steadfast love and faithfulness go before you" (Psalm 89:14). Whether the foundation of temple or house or the metaphorical foundation of a life, that foundation is the beginning point, the basis that determines if the product will withstand the onslaught of its life span.

Fruit

From Genesis through Revelation, the bearing of good fruit, literally and figuratively, is a primary goal of all life. The Genesis 1:11 passage, the first of 143 references to fruit, reads, "Then God said, 'Let the earth put forth vegetation: plants yielding seed, and fruit trees of every kind on earth that bear fruit with the seed in it.' And it was so."

25

The fruit image refers also to the human spirit, or, in the words of Christ, "The good person out of the good treasure of the heart produces good ..." (Luke 6:45). Paul defines this fruit: "By contrast, the fruit of the Spirit is love, joy, peace, patience, kindness, generosity, faithfulness, gentleness, and self-control" (Galatians 5:22-23a). See also Proverbs 12:12, Jeremiah 17:10, and John 4:36.

In the following verse from Colossians, Paul weds the three sections of today's passage. The solid foundation of knowledge gives vision and guides the heart toward bearing good fruit: "For this reason, since the day we heard it, we have not ceased praying for you and asking that you may *be filled with the knowledge of God's will in all spiritual wisdom and understanding, so that you may lead lives worthy of the Lord*, fully pleasing to him, *as you bear fruit in every good work* and *as you grow in the knowledge of God*" (Colossians 1:9-10).

Guide

"Guide" is a faith word, ours. The Psalms that use "guide" reassure. "You are indeed my rock and my fortress; for your name's sake lead me and guide me" (Psalm 31:3); "... [T]his is God ... will be our guide forever" (Psalm 48:14); "Let the nations be glad and sing for joy, for you judge the peoples with equity and guide the nations upon earth" (Psalm 67:4); and "You guide me with your counsel, and afterward you will receive me with honor" (Psalm 73:24). Among the more evocative passages about blindness and guides is Isaiah 43:16. (See "Chat Room" below.)

A "guide" or mentor presumes the requisite of trust: "[B]y springs of water [God] will guide them" (Isaiah 49:10); "The Lord will guide you continually, and satisfy your needs in parched places, and make your bones strong and you shall be like a watered garden, like a spring of water, whose waters never fail" (Isaiah 58:11); and "By the tender mercy of our God, the dawn from on high will break upon us, to give light to those who sit in darkness and in the shadow of death, to guide our feet into the way of peace" (Luke 1:78-79). Compared to these images of trustworthy guidance, the "blind guidance" of scribes and Pharisees embodies little of integrity.

26

Hypocrite

See Cycle C, Parable 10, Weather Signs.

4. Scripture Parallels

On The Blind Leading The Blind

"[Jesus] also told them a parable: 'Can a blind person guide a blind person? Will not both fall into a pit?'" (Luke 6:39). Matthew makes a statement of these questions. "And if one blind person guides another, both will fall into a pit."

Matthew prefaces this statement with another, referring to scribes and Pharisees: "Let them alone; they are blind guides of the blind" (Matthew 15:14). In Matthew 23:16-17, he refers to them as blind guides and as blind fools. See also Matthew 23:23-24.

A Disciple

The prefaces to the log and speck in the eye passages differ between Luke and Matthew. Luke leads with the blind leading the blind and the relationship between the disciple and the teacher. Matthew leads with words about judgment and measures. Later, Matthew addresses the material in Luke's preface: "A disciple is not above the teacher, but everyone who is fully qualified will be like the teacher" (Luke 6:40). Matthew also begins with "A disciple is not above the teacher" but adds "nor a slave above the master; it is enough for the disciple to be like the teacher, and the slave like the master" (Matthew 10:24-25a).

On Specks And Logs In The Eye

Wording of the Matthew 7:1-5 parallel is close to Luke 6. The initial question, "Why do you see the speck in your neighbor's eye, but do not notice the log in your own eye?" is the same. (See Luke 6:41 and Matthew 7:3.) The second question begins the same, "Or how can you say to your neighbor...?" However, Luke addresses the neighbor as "Friend" (Luke 6:42a).

Luke says, "let me take *out the speck*," where Matthew says, "let me take *the speck out*." Luke says, "*when you yourself do not see the log*," while Matthew says, *"while the log is in your own eye?"* (See Luke 6:42a and Matthew 7:4.)

The final line is identical in both versions: "You hypocrite, first take the log out of your own eye, and then you will see clearly to take the speck out of your neighbor's eye." (See Matthew 7:5 and Luke 6:42b.)

On Good Fruit And Bad Fruit

In earlier chapters of Matthew and Luke, the writers preface "good fruit" words from the same source. Both say, "Even now the ax is lying at the root of the trees; every tree therefore that does not bear good fruit is cut down and thrown into the fire" (Matthew 3:10 and Luke 3:9). Additionally, at the conclusion of his "good tree" passage, Matthew repeats, "Every tree that does not bear good fruit is cut down and thrown into the fire" (Matthew 7:19).

Regarding the recognition of false prophets, Matthew says, "You will know them by their fruits" (Matthew 7:16). Luke says, "No good tree bears bad fruit, nor again does a bad tree bear good fruit; for each tree is known by its own fruit" (Luke 6:43-44). Matthew speaks in a positive mode: "In the same way, every good tree bears good fruit, but the bad tree bears bad fruit" (Matthew 7:17), then repeats the message in the negative: "A good tree cannot bear bad fruit, nor can a bad tree bear good fruit" (Matthew 7:18).

Luke states, "Figs are not gathered from thorns, nor are grapes picked from a bramble bush" (Luke 6:44b), while Matthew employs the rhetorical question, "Are grapes gathered from thorns, or figs from thistles?" (Matthew 7:16b).

On Solid Learning

Luke prefaces this analogy with "Why do you call me 'Lord, Lord,' and do not do what I tell you? I will show you what someone is like who comes to me, hears my words, and acts on them" (Luke 6:46-48). Matthew's preface reads: "Everyone then who hears these words of mine and acts on them will be like a wise man who built his house on rock" (Matthew 7:24). Luke says, "who comes to me, hears my words, and acts on them," while Matthew says, "who hears these words of mine and acts on them."

"That one is like a man building a house, who dug deeply and laid the foundation on rock" (Luke 6:48a). Matthew says, "a wise man," and nothing about "the foundation." "Everyone then who hears these words of mine and acts on them will be like a wise man who built his house on rock" (Matthew 7:24).

"[W]hen a flood arose, the river burst against that house but could not shake it, because it had been well built" (Luke 6:48b). Matthew's description carries more drama: "The rain fell, the floods came, and the winds blew and beat on that house, but it did not fall, because it had been founded on rock" (Matthew 7:25).

"But the one who hears and does not act is like a man who built a house on the ground without a foundation" (Luke 6:49). Luke says, "one," and Matthew says, "everyone." Luke says, "who hears," and Matthew says, "who hears these words of mine."

Luke says, "a man," and Matthew says, "a foolish man." Luke says, "who built *a* house on the ground without a foundation," and Matthew says, "who built *his* house on sand." "And everyone who hears these words of mine and does not act on them will be like a foolish man who built his house on sand" (Matthew 7:26).

"When the river burst against it, immediately it fell, and great was the ruin of that house" (Luke 6:49b). Matthew goes into greater detail about the storm. Luke says, "immediately it fell," and Matthew says, "and it fell." Luke says, "and great was the ruin of that house" while Matthew says, "and great was its fall." "The rain fell, and the floods came, and the winds blew and beat against that house, and it fell — and great was its fall!" (Matthew 7:27).

5. Chat Room

Allison: What about seeing? I love Jesus' word play on seeing and not seeing in this passage. What a comment this trilogy of parables offers on our capacity to perceive, discern, and trust. Wow. Perception, insight, and eyesight; metaphorical blindness, short-sightedness, and long-distance perception; assessment of others, comprehension, and judgment; what do we know and how do we come to know it — they are all there.

29

Brenda: In contrast, as one who is blind, I smile at these words from a trustworthy guide: "I will lead the blind by a road they do not know, by paths they have not known I will guide them. I will turn the darkness before them into light, the rough places into level ground. These are the things I will do, and I will not forsake them" (Isaiah 42:16).

This is the one biblical passage wherein we who lack physical sight are given credit for being able to fend for ourselves. We hear the assumption that blindness is not totally incapacitating but only highly inconvenient. If God will lead "by unknown roads and paths," then there must also be routes that we do recognize and along which we do not need a human guide. This is possible. We walk parallel with the sound of moving traffic, count paces, and concentrate on nonvisual clues. Our feet perceive familiar changes in walking surface. Without a human guide, we use a mobility cane or dog guide.

Allison: As a seeing person, I cannot imagine one blind person guiding another blind person.

Brenda: Spoken like a true sighted person. I have done it while using a dog guide or a mobility cane as guide. With the other woman's hand grasping my elbow, we moved as a unit. However, I would avoid walking with a careless blind person.

Carol: I had a human guide once who was busy talking and forgot to allow for space for me. He veered to avoid a pothole and I stepped into it. It was then I decided to use my mobility cane whenever we went out together. Those who are unreliable should avoid guiding others. It does not build trust.

Brenda: Whether sighted or non-sighted, if you have the tools to know what you are doing, you can lead. If not, the person trusting your guidance can become as lost as the guide.

Allison: In these verses from Luke, Jesus moves from one topic to another in quick outline form. The trilogy reflects the complexity of his mind. It shows the intensity of Jesus' rush to teach much in a short time. It summarizes much that he has taught earlier.

Carol: Insight, or inner sight, goes a long way, doesn't it? Everything comes down to the wisdom of facing our own role of being responsible. After gaining as much wisdom about the workings of ourselves, then we can be capable teachers and effective guides of others. Similarly, as we learn, we must surround ourselves with the best guides.

Brenda: Somehow, I think Jesus went even further into our very being. Tend first to what is deepest within us. That influences everything that we do and all that we produce.

Allison: Back to the basics. Back to solid grounding and foundation. Everything Jesus counsels us is as solid as rock. We will go right if we listen to the insight of this guide and act upon what Jesus teaches.

---

1. For a discussion of this miracle, see "The Man Born Blind" in Brauninger, *Preaching The Miracles*, Series II, Cycle A (Lima, Ohio: CSS Publishing Co., Inc., 1998).

Parable 3

The Fruitless Fig Tree

Luke 13:1-9

---

1. Text

At that very time there were some present who told him about the Galileans whose blood Pilate had mingled with their sacrifices. [2] He asked them, "Do you think that because these Galileans suffered in this way they were worse sinners than all other Galileans? [3] No, I tell you; but unless you repent, you will all perish as they did. [4] Or those eighteen who were killed when the tower of Siloam fell on them — do you think that they were worse offenders than all the others living in Jerusalem? [5] No, I tell you; but unless you repent, you will all perish just as they did."

[6] Then he told this parable: "A man had a fig tree planted in his vineyard; and he came looking for fruit on it and found none. [7] So he said to the gardener, 'See here! For three years I have come looking for fruit on this fig tree, and still I find none. Cut it down! Why should it be wasting the soil?' [8] He replied, 'Sir, let it alone for one more year, until I dig around it and put manure on it. [9] If it bears fruit next year, well and good; but if not, you can cut it down.'"

2. What's Happening?

First Point Of Action

While Jesus is with the crowds, he hears about the Galileans whose blood Pilate had mingled with their sacrifices. Jesus asks two questions, giving the same response to each. Question A: Were these Galileans worse than all other Galileans because they suffered in this way? Question B: Were the eighteen who were killed when the tower of Siloam fell on them worse offenders than all the others living in Jerusalem?

Second Point Of Action

Jesus tells them that they will all perish as those did unless they repent.

Third Point Of Action

Jesus tells the crowds a parable, a conversation between a man and his gardener. A fig tree in the man's vineyard has not borne fruit for three years.

Fourth Point Of Action

The man tells his gardener to cut down this tree because it is wasting the soil.

Fifth Point Of Action

The gardener advises him to give it one more year. The gardener will dig around the tree and put manure on it.

3. Spadework

Fig Tree

While more than 800 species of fig exist, the common fig, *Ficus carica*, has been cultivated in the Mediterranean area since ancient times. Many fig species require five to seven years of growth before they begin to bear fruit. However, *F. carica* starts to bear at an early age, sometimes in the first year. Two crops of fruit are possible within the same season.

F. carica, classified as a shrub, grows fifteen to thirty feet in height. Another species of Mediterranean fig, *Ficus sycomorus,* is a taller tree, growing to fifty to seventy feet. This sycamore fig is favored in the Middle East for its shade. However, its fruit is inferior to the common fig. This is the true sycamore referred to four times in Hebrew texts and in the New Testament story about Zacchaeus. (See Luke 19:4.)

Twice in Hebrew Scripture, mention is made of creating cedars as "plentiful as sycamores," suggesting that the sycamore is easy to grow. (See 2 Chronicles 2:15 and 9:27.) By contrast, the fig tree appears 24 times throughout the entire Bible. Generally the fruit of the tree is also mentioned with these references.

Fig trees tend to fruit best when the soil is on the lean, dry side so that their vigor is restrained somewhat. A fig tree that makes excessively vigorous growth due to over-fertilization with nitrogen, as from nitrogen-rich manure, is likely to produce little or no fruit.

As an important symbol both of wealth and of the richness of the promised land, the fig tree was used as an object of God's pleasure or displeasure. The king of Assyria coaxed, "Make your peace with me and come out to me; then every one of you will eat from your own vine and your own fig tree, and drink water from your own cistern" (2 Kings 18:31).

As a further sign of God's displeasure with an errant people, God "struck their vines and fig trees, and shattered the trees of their country" (Psalm 105:33). "All their host shall wither like a leaf withering on a vine, or fruit withering on a fig tree" (Isaiah 34:4b). See also Jeremiah 8:13.

The fruitful fig tree or the barren "fig tree, the pomegranate, and the olive tree" all reflected God's pleasure or God's displeasure with the behavior of a nation or a people. See Haggai 2. Those who sat in the shade of a mature fig tree told of a time of prosperous peace. (See 1 Kings 4:25.)

A good tree does not bear bad fruit. A bad tree bears no good fruit. Following good plant husbandry, Christ said through Matthew, "Every tree that does not bear good fruit is cut down and thrown into the fire." (See Matthew 7:17-19.)

Everyone respected the owners and the gardeners of fig trees. "Anyone who tends a fig tree will eat its fruit, and anyone who takes care of a master will be honored" (Proverbs 27:18).

Repent

The powerful "repent" words (repented, repentance) are of lean use in the Bible. "Repent" occurs only eight times in Hebrew Scripture with no occurrences of "repentance." In the Gospels, each word occurs nine times. "Repented" appears four times in Hebrew Scripture and five times in the Gospels.

While use of "perish" and "destroy," the negative results of the choice not to repent, is heavy in Hebrew Scripture, their use also is light in the New Testament. Of the 135 instances of "perish" words (perish, perishes, perished) in the Bible, only nine appear in the New Testament. Luke uses these words in four references, two of which are in the present story.

Of the 449 instances of "destroy" words (destroy, destroys, destroyed, destruction), only 25 occur in the New Testament. Seven appear in Luke.

To feel enough remorse to turn around one's life is requisite to change, forgiveness, and salvation. Of the 112 references in scripture to the affirmative "forgive" words (forgive, forgives, forgiven, forgiveness), 57 appear in the New Testament. Of the 38 times "forgiven" is used, fourteen appear in the Gospels, all in Luke.

The sum of "save" words (save, saves, saved, saving, salvation) used in the Bible equals 408, a close second to the "destroy" words. Of these "save" words, 44 occur in the Gospels. Luke uses the "save" words in eighteen references.

The message of John the Baptist was "Repent, for the kingdom of heaven has come near" (Matthew 3:2). After his arrest, something changes in Jesus. (See Matthew 4:12-17.) "From that time," Matthew and Mark report, "Jesus began to proclaim, 'Repent, for the kingdom of heaven has come near' " (Matthew 4:17) and " 'The time is fulfilled, and the kingdom of God has come near; repent, and believe in the good news' " (Mark 1:15). Further, Jesus sends the disciples out to proclaim that all should repent. (See Mark 6:12.)

In the present Luke 13 story, Jesus' crisp clarity reflects another dimension of his complex character. He couples "repent" with the consequence of having failed to repent, "perish." Is this the harsh and urgent equivalent of today's "tough love"?

Repentance is the necessary confession. Forgiveness is the required response. (See Luke 17:4.) Compare this message with that found in 2 Peter: "The Lord is not slow about his promise, as some think of slowness, but is patient with you, not wanting any to perish, but all to come to repentance" (2 Peter 3:9).

Tower Of Siloam

Jesus refers in an almost off-handed manner to the incident of the eighteen people who were killed when the tower of Siloam fell on them. The prophet Isaiah speaks of the waters of Shiloah. (See Isaiah 8:6.) This name, along with Shiloa, is a variant of Siloam.

In the New Testament, Siloam is mentioned in relation to the pool of Siloam where Christ sent the man who was blind for healing. (See John 9:7ff.) In the preface to the parable of The Fruitless Fig Tree, the town tower is the focal point. Siloam, which the writer of John defines as Sent, is situated in the southwest corner of Jerusalem in the Kidron river valley not far from Jordan. The reservoir, or pool of Siloam, was an important agricultural water supply as it fed two irrigation channels.

A tower carried a double meaning. It was used both as a defense and as a symbol of the authority and power of religious and civic bodies, as shown in the following passages: "[F]or you are my refuge, a strong tower against the enemy" (Psalm 61:3); "But there was a strong tower within the city, and all the men and women and all the lords of the city fled to it and shut themselves in; and they went to the roof of the tower" (Judges 9:51); and "The name of the Lord is a strong tower; the righteous run into it and are safe" (Proverbs 18:10).

The destruction of the city tower that resulted in the death of eighteen people presented an untimely contradiction. Now, as then, towers that we once counted on for actual security and symbolic strength have become tenuous. Aside from the reference to the Siloam tower tragedy, Luke tells us nothing more.

4. Parallel Scripture

While this nature parable has no Gospel parallel, cross-references given below may offer further insight into its meaning.

On Repenting

"If one does not repent, God will whet his sword; he has bent and strung his bow" (Psalm 7:12). In contrast, see 2 Peter 3:9 above. This Peter passage portrays a patient God who, rather than destroy the unrepentant, is willing to wait for us to choose to repent.

Image Of The Faulty Fig Tree

"Even now the ax is lying at the root of the trees; every tree therefore that does not bear good fruit is cut down and thrown into the fire" (Matthew 3:10 and Luke 3:9). Threat of destruction again is present. In a season not ready for figs, the hungry Jesus causes the demise of a fig tree that did not provide him fruit. (See Matthew 21:18-20 and Mark 11:12-14.) Compare with Jeremiah 8:13, "When I wanted to gather them, says the Lord, there are no grapes on the vine, nor figs on the fig tree...." Are these references to a faulty fig tree indicative of an impatient and pressured Jesus or to the fulfilling of Hebrew Scripture?

The following morning according to the Gospel references, Jesus uses the example of the now-withered tree to remind the disciples that when they pray, "[I]f you do not doubt in your heart, but believe that what you say will come to pass, it will be done for you" (Mark 11:20-24).

Prestige Of Growing Fig Trees

Note the politics of the fig tree: "Do not listen to Hezekiah; for thus says the king of Assyria: 'Make your peace with me and come out to me; then everyone of you will eat from your own vine and your own fig tree and drink water from your own cistern' " (Isaiah 36:16). See also 2 Kings 18:31.

Let us note also the potentially esteemed relationship between the gardener and the owner: "Anyone who tends a fig tree will eat its fruit, and anyone who takes care of a master will be honored" (Proverbs 27:18).

5. Chat Room

The Gardener: "See here," my master said to me. "See here." He was angry. How many years have I been his gardener anyway? "See here," he said. Does he not trust me yet to do it right?

All I could answer was "Sir." I told him what I would do. You have to give these fig trees time. Most bear fruit quickly, some even within the same season. I like to give figs a fair chance — three, sometimes four years. Give them a little extra care, a little manure, a little cultivation. I know what I am doing, but he is the principal here. He is my superior.

Californian Farmer: That could mean if a fig tree is not any good, it does not make any difference what you would do to try to save it. Is not your master's point that if you or I have not shaped up by now, we never will?

It could also, of course, mean you as a gardener. I am unclear about your expertise as gardener. I farm here in southern California. We raise a different variety of fig here, but you certainly must know that figs do not appreciate the super rich soil that extra manure would provide.

Something might have been amiss with your care if there was a need to weed around the fig. I wondered at first if your suggestion of weeding and manure was a remedy for negligence on your part.

Perhaps your offer to cultivate and fertilize was a desperate attempt to assure the fig tree owner that you know what you are doing. Even you agreed to cut down the fig if it did not produce in another year.

Gardener: It was my patience against his impatience. Did you notice that he said nothing after I offered to cultivate and fertilize?

Anonymous: Greetings. I have been following your chat. Did your master in fact leave the conversation unfinished? I do not think so. I suspect the look on his face was final. If you are not productive, slash. If you are not working to expectations within a certain time

39

frame, slash. Do not waste our time or space. If your advancing age causes you to work at a slower pace, leave. We will replace you.

California: The human soul constantly needs tending. What happened to the God we know who is accepting? That God is ready to give us one more chance.

Anonymous: It hinges on the word, "unless." Unless you change your ways, it will be too late for you. Christ said it twice. With that little word, all the doom turns around to hope.

Here are several questions for anybody else out there in cyberspace. Who is this Jesus who scares the wits out of us by reminding us not only of one but two horrible things that happened to the Galileans? Why did he bring up the suffering of the Galileans at Pilate's hand? Why did he remind the crowd of the eighteen who were killed when the Tower of Siloam fell?

Joseph of Siloam: I can respond to that. I am Joseph of Siloam. Remember that some among those gathered told Jesus about the deaths of the Galileans. For all I know, this was the first that Jesus had heard about it.

Maybe his response to that suffering was to recall another catastrophe. To cite the senseless deaths of the eighteen innocents from our town may have been a natural human response, a ticking off of the calamities. Jesus' response may have been a sign of the pressure Jesus felt to get his job done.

John of Galilee: Jesus' mention of the tower tragedy did appear to be almost off the cuff. He said, *"Or those eighteen...."* But the memory was a common bond, never to be forgotten. Jesus need not have said anything else to be understood.

Jesus did appear pressed. He was serious, solemn. He raised his voice at the rampant hypocrisy of leadership. He had a message for change and would use whatever illustration was at hand.

Joseph of Siloam: How ironic that the very place we flocked to for safety, our town tower, would become a place of death. I ponder if everything that happens to us is causal? Is everything ultimately our fault? Is everything retribution? What is by chance and what is by design? How much, indeed, are we in control of our own lives?

Anonymous: That does not sound like the Jesus I know. His words suggest that all of us, even the innocent, need to change our ways. Everyone needs to change. We are human. We stray from the intended course. Yet, we know the deaths of the eighteen had nothing to do with a greater or lesser degree of alienation from God or each other or themselves. The tragedy happened and they just happened to be there.

Joseph of Siloam: Jesus startled us. "Unless you repent, you will perish," he was trying to tell us. The tower was a cryptic image of death. He leashed my attention. Then Jesus remembered himself and told a story. You know how it is. You try to tell folk something straight out, but they do not get it. Then you catch their attention with a story. Jesus knew that worked.

California: Jesus' words are harsh. I want God to give me another chance forever. I slough off, but I keep trying. If I felt that God ever would give up on me, I would give up on myself. I hope we do not have to follow that fig tree parable to the letter. Were I a living plant, I would want some gardener to have enough faith in my possibility not to give up on me. I cannot thrive under a shadow of fear. I need hope.

Anonymous: This is a difficult parable for us to hear. Who wins here, the owner of the fig tree or the gardener?

California: Well, I of course want the garden to win. It is the gardener who has hope, who knows what the fig needs. I am practical enough to know, however, that some figs must come out. The plant is no good.

Anonymous: On another level, what does it take to nurture a church to bear fruit? When should we call it quits and close the doors? What does it take for us to change to productive living? What does this parable say about God and God's faith in us?

Joseph of Siloam: This parable does reach far beyond my town. This wonderful story is about compromise — about having a dream, realizing that this dream might not come to fruition, setting limits as to how long you are going to pursue your dream, and having the flexibility and the courage to change course if need be. It is about making choices and living with the outcome.

Anonymous: I agree that the parable addresses compromise. It also expands my concept of God and God's role in my life.

California: Tell us more.

Anonymous: I tend to over-simplify the creator, but God is too complex to slip into categories. God is the landowner with the capacity to grasp the whole setting. God is the one who has high expectations and who requires results. God also is the nurturing gardener who cares for each part of creation with such intensity that God will extend hope as far as possible. Maybe God is also that fig tree, for without the right mix of circumstances, God's plans cannot come to fruition.

California: I too am a composite of seeming opposites. I am both the gardener and the landowner, sometimes in conflict and sometimes finding harmony. Unlike God, however, I need to turn away from my wrongdoing before it becomes my irreparable undoing.

Parable 4

The Prodigal Sons

Luke 15:1-3, 11-32

---

1. Text

*Now all the tax collectors and sinners were coming near
to listen to him. [2] And the Pharisees and the scribes
were grumbling and saying, "This fellow welcomes sinners and eats with them."*

[3] So he told them this parable:

*Then Jesus said, "There was a man who had two
sons. [12] The younger of them said to his father, 'Father, give me the share of the property that will belong
to me.' So he divided his property between them. [13] A
few days later the younger son gathered all he had and
traveled to a distant country, and there he squandered
his property in dissolute living. [14] When he had spent
everything, a severe famine took place throughout that
country, and he began to be in need. [15] So he went
and hired himself out to one of the citizens of that country, who sent him to his fields to feed the pigs. [16] He
would gladly have filled himself with the pods that the
pigs were eating; and no one gave him anything. [17]
But when he came to himself he said, 'How many of my
father's hired hands have bread enough and to spare,
but here I am dying of hunger! [18] I will get up and go
to my father, and I will say to him, "Father, I have sinned
against heaven and before you; [19] I am no longer
worthy to be called your son; treat me like one of your
hired hands."' [20] So he set off and went to his father.*

But while he was still far off, his father saw him and was filled with compassion; he ran and put his arms around him and kissed him. [21] Then the son said to him, 'Father, I have sinned against heaven and before you; I am no longer worthy to be called your son.' [22] But the father said to his slaves, 'Quickly, bring out a robe — the best one — and put it on him; put a ring on his finger and sandals on his feet. [23] And get the fatted calf and kill it, and let us eat and celebrate; [24] for this son of mine was dead and is alive again; he was lost and is found!' And they began to celebrate.

[25] "Now his elder son was in the field; and when he came and approached the house, he heard music and dancing. [26] He called one of the slaves and asked what was going on. [27] He replied, 'Your brother has come, and your father has killed the fatted calf, because he has got him back safe and sound.' [28] Then he became angry and refused to go in. His father came out and began to plead with him. [29] But he answered his father, 'Listen! For all these years I have been working like a slave for you, and I have never disobeyed your command; yet you have never given me even a young goat so that I might celebrate with my friends. [30] But when this son of yours came back, who has devoured your property with prostitutes, you killed the fatted calf for him!' [31] Then the father said to him, 'Son, you are always with me, and all that is mine is yours. [32] But we had to celebrate and rejoice, because this brother of yours was dead and has come to life; he was lost and has been found.'"

2. What's Happening?

First Point Of Action
A statement by the Pharisees and scribes prompts this parable.

Second Point Of Action
The younger sibling demands and ill-uses his inheritance.

Third Point Of Action
His life in the real world brings the son to reality.

Fourth Point Of Action
The son decides to return to his father.

Fifth Point Of Action
The father responds with compassion.

Sixth Point Of Action
The elder sibling responds to the celebration.

Seventh Point Of Action
The elder sibling and the father engage in conversation.

3. Spadework

Dissolute Living
Amoral, wanton, unethical, godless, loose, weak, and wild behavior — everything that is the opposite of virtuous, moral, and righteous characterizes dissolute living. Dissolute living is a deliberate and chosen lifestyle of negative energy rather than the result alone of innocence or immaturity.

A play upon a similar word, "dissolution," suggests that dissolute behavior is not part of the solution. It contributes to brokenness rather than to wholeness. It fragments the heart rather than binds our whole being together. It destroys rather than nurtures relationships. It brings about endings rather than life beginnings. Dissolute living is about the falling apart, disintegration, and crumbling of the human spirit rather than a life that blossoms with the vigor of spiritual health.

Fatted Calf
"Fatted calf" refers to the best that one has to offer. "Calf" occurs 23 times in the Bible. Fatted calf, however, appears on only one other occasion. In 1 Samuel, when the woman saw that Saul was terrified at the prospect of facing the Philistines, she prepared

him food to give him strength for the journey. (See 1 Samuel 28: 19-25.) "Now the woman had a fatted calf in the house. She quickly slaughtered it, and she took flour, kneaded it, and baked unleavened cakes" (1 Samuel 28: 24).

Give Me

From Genesis 14:21 to Revelation 10:9, "Give me" appears 76 times, whereas "Give us" occurs in 23 instances. What is the negotiation between the giver and the receiver? Is there an implicit expectation of being given something in return, or is "Give me" always one-directional?

Give me is that demanding of or begging from one person to another. It "thingifies" rather than humanizes. What does it take for us to make the request, "Give me"? How can we judge what is right for us? The Give me of what we "have coming to us," that is, human rights, justice, and equality, is non-negotiable.

How do the Give me's that we ask of God differ from those we request or demand of others? "The younger of [the siblings] said to his father, 'Father, give me the share of the property that will belong to me.' So he divided his property between them" (Luke 15:12). When do we graduate from the gimme's to that other Give me?

"*Give me* understanding, that I may keep your law and observe it with my whole heart" (Psalm 119:34). "Your hands have made and fashioned me; *give me* understanding that I may learn your commandments" (Psalm 11:73). "I am your servant; *give me* understanding, so that I may know your decrees" (Psalm 119:125).

Hope Of Forgiveness

Christ suggests that despite our inability to avoid sinning, there is hope for sinners: "Just so, I tell you, there is joy in the presence of the angels of God over one sinner who repents" (Luke 15:10). For Christ and for God, people still count one by one. "Just so, I tell you, there will be more joy in heaven over one sinner who repents than over ninety-nine righteous persons who need no repentance" (Luke 15:7).

Christ wants all members of the human family to be people of hope rather than of despair. God's generous attitude toward sin influences our posture in our relationships with others. "Then Peter came and said to him, 'Lord, if another member of the church sins against me, how often should I forgive? As many as seven times?' Jesus said to him, 'Not seven times, but, I tell you, seventy-seven times' " (Matthew 18:21-22).

Earlier, Hebrew Prophets also spoke of redemption: "I, I am He who blots out your transgressions for my own sake, and I will not remember your sins" (Isaiah 43:25). "I have swept away your transgressions like a cloud, and your sins like mist; return to me, for I have redeemed you" (Isaiah 44:22). "But if the wicked turn away from all their sins that they have committed and keep all my statutes and do what is lawful and right, they shall surely live; they shall not die" (Ezekiel 18:21).

Psalm 103 must have influenced the attitude of Christ toward forgiveness:

> *The Lord is merciful and gracious,*
> *slow to anger and abounding in steadfast love.*
> *He will not always accuse,*
> *nor will he keep his anger forever.*
> *He does not deal with us according to our sins,*
> *nor repay us according to our iniquities.*
> *For as the heavens are high above the earth,*
> *so great is his steadfast love toward those who fear him;*
> *as far as the east is from the west,*
> *so far he removes our transgressions from us.*
> — Psalm 103:8-12

Can we ask for forgiveness before we know that we will be forgiven? Is knowing that God will forgive us what empowers our capacity to change our path and ask for forgiveness? What promotes being acceptable, feeling acceptable? Something miraculous within the despair of hopelessness turns us around in the direction of hope. Perhaps we first recognize that change within us when we begin to consider that we need forgiveness. Perhaps that cognizance is the seed of God's steadfast love within us.

47

Pharisee

For a discussion of Pharisee, see Cycle C, Parable 18, Two Men At Prayer.

Sin, Sinner(s)

Six of the fifteen biblical references to "sinner" appear in Luke. The initial reference, however, occurs in 1 Samuel 2:25. Of 24 references to "sinners" in the New Testament, fourteen occur in the Gospels. Twelve relate to Jesus' association with tax collectors and sinners.

"Sin" occurs 73 times in the New Testament. In the Gospels, "sin" is used sixteen times, all, with one exception, are words of Christ. Sin appears on 227 occasions in Hebrew Scripture. References in Exodus 16:1 and 17:1 name a "wilderness of Sin" situated between Elim and Sinai. Here, the thirsty and hungry Israelites complained to Moses and Aaron, wishing they had died while still in Egypt. Here, where they camped after setting out from the Red Sea, God sent manna from heaven to feed the wandering Israelites. Here also, God later instructed Moses to strike the rock out of which would come water at Horeb. (See also Numbers 33:11-12.)

Of 158 biblical references to "sins," seventy occur in the New Testament. Of the 23 Gospel occurrences, "sins" appears thirteen times in Luke, nine in Matthew, and seven in Mark.

Sinner (Definition)

A definition of a sinner begins to emerge as one surveys scripture. In the Hebrew Scripture, sin involves provoking God by doing what is evil in God's sight: "Then I lay prostrate before the Lord as before, forty days and forty nights; I neither ate bread nor drank water, because of all the sin you had committed, provoking the Lord by doing what was evil in his sight" (Deuteronomy 9:18).

Among the clearest descriptions of sin is this from James: "But one is tempted by one's own desire, being lured and enticed by it; then, when that desire has conceived, it gives birth to sin, and that sin, when it is fully grown, gives birth to death" (James 1:14-15). The writer of James understands a sinner as one who is "wandering." "[Y]you should know that whoever brings back a sinner from wandering will save the sinner's soul from death and will cover a multitude of sins" (James 5:20). The writer of James further paints sin as showing partiality (while loving your neighbor as yourself). (See James 2:8-9.)

The author of Romans views sinning as being disobedient "For just as by the one man's disobedience the many were made sinners, so by the one man's obedience the many will be made righteous" (Romans 5:19).

The writer of Matthew suggests that the human causes of sin can be removed and that sinning and doing evil are related. "The Son of Man will send his angels, and they will collect out of his kingdom all causes of sin and all evildoers" (Matthew 13:41ff).

Contrasting the learned with common folk who might know little, the man whom Jesus heals of blindness counters the Pharisees' attempts to label Christ as a sinner. The man speaks truth. "So for the second time they called the man who had been blind, and they said to him, 'Give glory to God! We know that this man is a sinner.' He answered, 'I do not know whether he is a sinner. One thing I do know, that though I was blind, now I see' " (John 9:24-25).

The words of Christ in the Gospel of John suggest that sin is universal to the human family. "When they kept on questioning him, he straightened up and said to them, 'Let anyone among you who is without sin be the first to throw a stone at [the woman caught in committing adultery]' " (John 8:7).

From the first of John's letters come three commentaries on sin: "Everyone who commits sin is guilty of lawlessness; sin is lawlessness" (1 John 3:4). "Everyone who commits sin is a child of the devil; for the devil has been sinning from the beginning. The Son of God was revealed for this purpose, to destroy the works of the devil" (1 John 3:8). "We know that those who are born of God do not sin, but the one who was born of God protects them, and the evil one does not touch them" (1 John 5:18).

In the book of Romans, sin is an entity separate from the existence of the law: "Therefore, just as sin came into the world through one man, and death came through sin, and so death spread to all because all have sinned — sin was indeed in the world before the law, but sin is not reckoned when there is no law" (Romans 5:12-13). However, were it not for the law, one might not recognize sin: "What then should we say? That the law is sin? By no means! Yet, if it had not been for the law, I would not have known sin. I would not have known what it is to covet if the law had not said, 'You shall not covet' " (Romans 7:7). The author of Romans further defines sin as "whatever does not proceed from faith." See Romans 14:23.

Sin is "the devising of folly" (Proverbs 24:9). Sin is exercised with the tongue. "I will keep a muzzle on my mouth as long as the wicked are in my presence." (See Psalm 39:1.)

Tax Collector(s)

Jesus counsels the tax collectors: "Even tax collectors came to be baptized, and they asked him, 'Teacher, what should we do?' He said to them, 'Collect no more than the amount prescribed for you' " (Luke 3:12-13).

Jesus quotes his opponents: " '[T]he Son of Man came eating and drinking, and they say, "Look, a glutton and a drunkard, a friend of tax collectors and sinners!" Yet wisdom is vindicated by her deeds.' "(Matthew 11:19). See also Luke 7:34. When the chief priests and elders question Jesus about this matter in the temple, Jesus retorts, " 'Truly I tell you, the tax collectors and the prostitutes are going into the kingdom of God ahead of you' " (Matthew 21:31b).

Five of the seven New Testament references to "tax collector" occur in Luke. The other two are in Matthew. Six references to "tax collectors" appear in Matthew, three in Mark, and six in Luke. Zacchaeus was a tax collector (Luke 19:2), as were Levi who dropped everything to follow Christ (Luke 5:27) and the disciple, Matthew (Matthew 10:3).

4. Parallel Scriptures

The parable of the Prodigal Sons is special to the writer of Luke.

Found

Of the 312 biblical references to "found," only a few refer to the state of being found, that is, of finding reconciliation with one's self, family, and God. The following passages are worthy of consideration in light of those who are prodigal:

"And you, my son Solomon, know the God of your father, and serve him with single mind and willing heart; for the Lord searches every mind, and understands every plan and thought. If you seek him, he will be *found* by you; but if you forsake him, he will abandon you forever" (1 Chronicles 28:9). See also 2 Chronicles 15:2 and these words spoken to King Jehoshaphat, "Nevertheless, some good is *found* in you, for you ... have set your heart to seek God" (2 Chronicles 19:3).

Several Hebrew writers speak of the godless, who will not be found: "They will fly away like a dream, and not be found; they will be chased away like a vision of the night. The eye that saw them will see them no more, nor will their place behold them any longer" (Job 20:8-9). Ezekiel says, "I will bring you to a dreadful end, and you shall be no more; though sought for, you will never be found again, says the Lord God" (Ezekiel 26:21). From Daniel, "Then he shall turn back toward the fortresses of his own land, but he shall stumble and fall, and shall not be found" (Daniel 11:19).

The following words from Isaiah may well have been the morning and evening prayer of the father in the parable of the prodigals:

> *Seek the Lord while he may be found,*
> *call upon him while he is near;*
> *let the wicked forsake their way,*
> *and the unrighteous their thoughts;*
> *let them return to the Lord, that he may have mercy on*
>   *them,*
> *and to our God, for he will abundantly pardon.*
> *For my thoughts are not your thoughts,*
> *nor are your ways my ways, says the Lord.*
> — Isaiah 55:6-8

Like the father's " '... rejoice, because ... he was lost and has been found' " (Luke 15:32), the finder of the lost sheep and the

51

finder of the lost coin utter similar words: " 'Rejoice with me, for I have found my sheep that was lost' " (Luke 15:5-6) and " 'Rejoice with me, for I have found the coin that I had lost' " (Luke 15:9). (See Cycle C, Parable 13, Lost And Found.)

Lost

Compare the two mentions of "lost and found" in the present parable, " '[F]or this son of mine was dead and is alive again; he was lost and is found!' And they began to celebrate" (Luke 15:24) and " '[b]ut we had to celebrate and rejoice, because this brother of yours was dead and has come to life; he was lost and has been found' " (Luke 15:32) with the following "lost and found" passages: (1) "Just so, I tell you, there will be more joy in heaven over one sinner who repents than over ninety-nine righteous persons who need no repentance" (Luke 15:7) and (2) "Just so, I tell you, there is joy in the presence of the angels of God over one sinner who repents" (Luke 15:10).

Among several Hebrew texts that refer to a lost inner state of well being are the following four passages: (1) "I have gone astray like a lost sheep; seek out your servant, for I do not forget your commandments" (Psalm 119:176); (2) "They die for lack of discipline, and because of their great folly they are lost" (Proverbs 5:23); (3) "And I said: 'Woe is me! I am lost, for I am a man of unclean lips, and I live among a people of unclean lips; yet my eyes have seen the King, the Lord of hosts!' " (Isaiah 6:5); and (4) "My people have been lost sheep; their shepherds have led them astray, turning them away on the mountains; from mountain to hill they have gone, they have forgotten their fold" (Jeremiah 50:6).

Jesus is quoted infrequently as using "lost" in the sense of relationship with self and God: "These twelve Jesus sent out with the following instructions: 'Go nowhere among the Gentiles, and enter no town of the Samaritans, but go rather to the lost sheep of the house of Israel' " (Matthew 10:5-6). Jesus also responded, "But he did not answer her at all. And his disciples came and urged him, saying, 'Send her away, for she keeps shouting after us.' He answered, 'I was sent only to the lost sheep of the house of Israel' " (Matthew 15:23-24). Also according to the writer of Matthew, Jesus said, "So it is not the will of your Father in heaven that one of these little ones should be lost" (Matthew 18:14).

In addition to the "lost and found" of the parable about the prodigals, the juxtaposition of lost with found is also used in the lost and found parables of the lost sheep and the lost coin that precede the present parable. These parables are found in Luke 15:4-10 (Cycle C, Parable 14).

Property

The younger sibling referred to "the share of the property that will belong to [him]" (Luke 15:12). Hebrew texts refer to allotted property: "You must not move your neighbor's boundary marker, set up by former generations, on *the property that will be allotted to you* in the land that the Lord your God is giving you to possess" (Deuteronomy 19:14) and "Jeremiah set out from Jerusalem to go to the land of Benjamin *to receive his share of property* among the people there" (Jeremiah 37:12).

One can find "squandered property" both in the present parable and in that of the Clever Crook, also in Luke. "Then Jesus said to the disciples, 'There was a rich man who had a manager, and charges were brought to him that this man was *squandering his property*'" (Luke 16:1). See "The Clever Crook," Cycle C, Parable 14. The third instance of "squander" in the Bible occurs in Proverbs 29:3: "A child who loves wisdom makes a parent glad, but to keep company with prostitutes is to *squander* one's substance."

Tax Collectors

In Luke 15:1-3, when the Pharisees question Jesus about eating with tax collectors and sinners, Jesus answers with the parable of the family. In Matthew, Jesus responds, " 'Those who are well have no need of a physician, but those who are sick' " (Matthew 9:12). According to Mark, Jesus' response was, "Those who are well have no need of a physician, but those who are sick; I have come to call not the righteous but sinners." (Mark 2:17). In Luke 5:31-32, the words duplicate Mark's with the addition of "to repentance" after "sinners."

5. Chat Room

Older Child: Dad's words kept echoing in the days and weeks after you returned home, kid. "We *had* to celebrate," Dad said. I took issue with his generosity. I thought I was the mature one. I was not mature. I was just established.

Younger Child: All I knew was I had to get out of there. You had everything. You have the business smarts. You can work with Pop.

Older Child: You can, too. You just have to anticipate him a little — his moods, when he is getting tired, keep the inflow and the outflow balanced. You know.

Younger Child: That's what I mean. You can read him. You and I are put together differently. There was no room for me. You two are a team. He respects your suggestions. He didn't even hear me when I tried to tell him something.

Older Child: You and Dad are a lot like each other. In a strange sort of way, you are the one with the insight, kid. To be honest, you understood the firstborn's relationship with the father better than I did. I felt only that it was my responsibility as the elder one, my duty. My partnership was not a matter of choice.

Younger Child: I thought it would be so easy. I'd have my inheritance and go out on my own. Then all of a sudden I was as stuck as I had been at home. The money was gone. I was without a job. I found myself without everything. I found myself.

Older Child: What happened, anyway?

Younger Child: It was great to be free. I didn't really know what I was going to do. I didn't have to worry. I had the inheritance. I could play for a long time, see new places, do some things before I had to start thinking about the stodgy stuff.

Older Child: Like not playing all of your funds on stocks?

Younger Child: Diversify. See, I should have listened to you, there, too. I was too ashamed to come home to Pop and Mom. I tried out everything that tempted me. I was too embarrassed by my actions not to come home. I had to return to who I was. Pop and Mom had taught us both what is wrong and what is right.

Older Child: But you came home. When they told me what you said to Dad, I thought at first you were just trying to play with him again. How could he take you back? Would he also give you my part of the inheritance now? That ring should have been mine.

Younger Child: I was not looking for money. You said you kept hearing Pop say he *had* to celebrate. Well, I *had* to come home and apologize to Pop. I had lost the right to be called his son.

Only now do I see that coming home was the one chance, the only chance I would have to start all over again. Pop owes me nothing, I owe him everything.

Older Child: Hi, Dad.

Younger Child: I did not expect you to wrap your arms around me, Pop.

Father: And you did not expect me to celebrate. That is what "cherish" means, son. By adoption or by birth, you are my children. You are my beloved. When you, my firstborn, find routine tedious, I wait for you to discover for yourself the creative orifices of stability. I teach you all I know about my life work. I wait for you to appreciate the responsibility of partnership as well as to sludge through the responsibility of knowing that my existence is short-lived. By nature, you are a steady-at-the-helm person.

And you, my younger child, will come to sense that my letting you go with my blessing and with your part of the property exemplified my love for you. More than anything else, you needed freedom to explore, to make your mistakes, and to find yourself. When you have daughters and sons yourself, you will fully understand both my sorrow and my hope for you in your time of wandering absence.

You are two individuals. Nothing either of you could do is stronger than my love for you. Nothing. I could, indeed, do nothing other than celebrate your return. As happens to all of God's creation, you were lost, and now you are found. Welcome home, both of you, my beloved children.

Parable 5

Two Men In Debt

Luke 7:36-50

---

1. Text

One of the Pharisees asked Jesus to eat with him, and he went into the Pharisee's house and took his place at the table. [37] And a woman in the city, who was a sinner, having learned that he was eating in the Pharisee's house, brought an alabaster jar of ointment. [38] She stood behind him at his feet, weeping, and began to bathe his feet with her tears and to dry them with her hair. Then she continued kissing his feet and anointing them with the ointment. [39] Now when the Pharisee who had invited him saw it, he said to himself, "If this man were a prophet, he would have known who and what kind of woman this is who is touching him — that she is a sinner." [40] Jesus spoke up and said to him, "Simon, I have something to say to you." "Teacher," he replied, "Speak." [41] "A certain creditor had two debtors; one owed five hundred denarii, and the other fifty. [42] When they could not pay, he canceled the debts for both of them. Now which of them will love him more?" [43] Simon answered, "I suppose the one for whom he canceled the greater debt." And Jesus said to him, "You have judged rightly." [44] Then turning toward the woman, he said to Simon, "Do you see this woman? I entered your house; you gave me no water for my feet, but she has bathed my feet with her tears and dried them with her hair. [45] You gave me no kiss, but from the time I came in she has not stopped kissing my feet. [46]

57

You did not anoint my head with oil, but she has anointed my feet with ointment. [47] Therefore, I tell you, her sins, which were many, have been forgiven; hence she has shown great love. But the one to whom little is forgiven, loves little." [48] Then he said to her, "Your sins are forgiven." [49] But those who were at the table with him began to say among themselves, "Who is this who even forgives sins?" [50] And he said to the woman, "Your faith has saved you; go in peace."

2. What's Happening?

First Point Of Action
A Pharisee asks Jesus to eat with him. Jesus enters the house, taking his place at the table.

Second Point Of Action
An unnamed woman in the city, who is a sinner, learns about this and brings him an alabaster jar of ointment.

Third Point Of Action
She stands behind Jesus at his feet. She weeps, bathing his feet with her tears, and wipes them with her hair. She kisses his feet and anoints them with ointment.

Fourth Point Of Action
Observing this, the host says to himself that if "the man" were a prophet, he would have known who and what kind of woman was touching him.

Fifth Point Of Action
Jesus addresses Simon by name, telling him he has something to say to him. With two words, Simon calls him, "Teacher," and says, "Speak."

Sixth Point Of Action
Jesus tells the parable of the creditor and the two men in debt. One debtor owed 500 denarii and the other 50 denarii. When they could not pay, the creditor canceled both debts.

58

Seventh Point Of Action

Jesus asks Simon which debtor will love the creditor more. When Simon chooses the debtor with the greater debt, Jesus says he judged correctly.

Eighth Point Of Action

Turning his attention toward the woman's actions, Jesus compares his host's hospitality with that of the woman. Simon gave him no water for his feet and no kiss and did not anoint his head with oil. The woman bathed his feet with her tears and dried them with her hair. She has not stopped kissing his feet from the time Jesus came in. Then she anointed his feet with oil.

Ninth Point Of Action

Making an analogy with the debtors and creditor, Jesus says her sins which were many were forgiven. That is the reason she has shown great love. The one to whom little is forgiven, loves little, Jesus says.

Tenth Point Of Action

Addressing the woman, Jesus tells her that her sins are forgiven.

Eleventh Point Of Action

Others at the table, presumably Pharisees, talk among themselves wondering who this is who even forgives sins.

Twelfth Point Of Action

Jesus continues speaking to the woman. He tells her that her faith has saved her and instructs her to go in peace.

3. Spadework

Alabaster[1]

In addition to mention in the three versions of this story told in the Synoptic Gospels, alabaster appears in Song of Songs to describe the legs of the beloved one: "His legs are alabaster columns, set upon bases of gold" (Song of Solomon 5:15a).

One can presume that the ointment in this jar was costly because alabaster jars were saved for the finest perfume. Therefore, the mention of "very costly" ointment in the parallel stories as recorded by the writers of Matthew and Mark drew even greater attention to the dearness of the woman's gift.

Alabaster flasks were imported from Egypt in the form of small objects. They were bored with a drill, while flasks made in Palestine from native gypsum from the Jordan Valley were hollowed out with a chisel. Easily broken, the light cream-colored and veined stone is soft enough to scratch with a fingernail.

Anoint (-ed, -ing)

Several of the 27 references in Hebrew Scripture refer to the anointing of Aaron, a priestly ordination and consecration, by pouring oil over his turbaned head. (See Exodus 28:41, 29:5-8, 30:30, 40:13, and 40:15.) Other priests, kings, and prophets also were anointed. (See 1 Samuel 9:16, 15:1, 16:3, and 16:12-13; 1 Kings 1:34 and 19:15; and 2 Kings 9:6 and 9:12.)

However, "sacred anointing oil" was used only for holy anointing of persons and sacred religious objects and places. For a recipe for "sacred anointing oil" made by a perfumer from liquid myrrh, sweet-smelling cinnamon, aromatic cane, cassia, and olive oil, see Exodus 30:22-33.

An additional 26 references use "anointing oil" or "anointing." Was this holy, consecrating oil understood to have special power? Moses told Aaron and his two sons, "You shall not go outside the entrance of the tent of meeting, or you will die; for the anointing oil of the Lord is on you" (Leviticus 10:7). "Do not touch my anointed ones; do my prophets no harm" (1 Chronicles 16:22 and Psalm 105:15). Among the ninety references to "anointed," one finds several phrased as "the Lord's anointed," "his anointed," and "my anointed one."

Olive oil was used for general anointing of the body. (See Deuteronomy 28:40, Judges 9:8, and Ruth 3:3.) Women in mourning did not anoint themselves. (See 2 Samuel 14:2.) Animals were anointed before a sacrificial offering. (See Exodus 29:36.)

Consider this verse in light of today's parable wherein love overflowed with the anointing of Jesus' feet as he sat at the dinner table in the presence of enemies: "You prepare a table before me in the presence of my enemies; you anoint my head with oil; my cup overflows" (Psalm 23:5).

As impractical as it may have seemed, the woman treasured the ointment and did not further waste it by wiping it off with a towel. She used her hair, which also benefitted from the oil.

In addition to the anointing passages in the Synoptic Gospels that refer to today's parable and parallel scripture, the following passages are of interest: "When the sabbath was over, Mary Magdalene, and Mary the mother of James, and Salome bought spices, so that they might go and *anoint* him" (Mark 16:1); "[The disciples] cast out many demons, and *anointed with oil* many who were sick and cured them" (Mark 6:13); and "[The disciple Andrew] first found his brother Simon and said to him, 'We have found the Messiah' (which is translated *Anointed*)" (John 1:41).

Also of note is the passage from the Isaiah scroll that Jesus was given to read in the synagogue upon returning to Nazareth after the temptations in the wilderness: "The Spirit of the Lord is upon me, because he has *anointed me* to bring good news to the poor. He has sent me to proclaim release to the captives and recovery of sight to the blind, to let the oppressed go free" (Luke 4:18 quoting Isaiah 61:1).

Feet/Kiss

The initial mention of feet, the first of 216 references, was Abraham's offering of a kindness, a standard act of hospitality after a hot, dusty journey to God, who came as three men. "Let a little water be brought, and wash your feet, and rest yourselves under the tree" (Genesis 18:4). The offer to wash feet was also an invitation to come into the house and stay awhile. (See 2 Samuel 11:8ff.)

Scripture suggests that travelers washed their own hot and sweaty feet. However, when David sent news to Abigail by way of his servants that he wished to have her as his wife, she "rose and bowed down, with her face to the ground, and said, 'Your servant

61

is a slave to wash the feet of the servants of my lord' " (1 Samuel 25:41).

To kiss someone's well-traveled feet was obeisance at its best: "Now therefore, O kings, be wise; / be warned, O rulers of the earth. / Serve the Lord with fear, / with trembling kiss his feet, / or he will be angry, and you will perish in the way; / for his wrath is quickly kindled" (Psalm 2:10-12). See also Isaiah 49:23, "Kings ... and their queens ... With their faces to the ground they shall bow down to you, and lick the dust of your feet. Then you will know that I am the Lord; those who wait for me shall not be put to shame."

Luke 9:5 and 10:11 refer to shaking the dust of the town off one's feet. Several references relate to a submissive position at Jesus' feet. In addition to Luke 7:28 and 7:44, see Matthew 15:30 and 22:44; Mark 5:22, 7:25, and 12:36; and Luke 8:35, 8:41, 10:39, and 17:16.

Jesus washed the feet of his disciples. Peter was embarrassed when Jesus began to wash his feet. Jesus explained that "servants are not greater than their master, nor are messengers greater than the one who sent them" (John 13:16).

Judas betrayed Jesus with a kiss. (See Matthew 26:48, Mark 14:44, and Luke 22:47.)

"Go In Peace"

This phrase is used eleven times. The first, from Exodus, has a permissive rather than a formulaic tone: "Moses went back to his father-in-law Jethro and said to him, 'Please let me go back to my kindred in Egypt and see whether they are still living.' And Jethro said to Moses, 'Go in peace' " (Exodus 4:18). Its use in the present parable also has a personal, non-formulaic tone.

The priest told the Levite, Eli told Hannah, and Jonathan told David to go in peace. All three narrators add a God-connection ("under the eye of God," "the God of Israel grant," and "in the name of the Lord") as if the words contained also the blessing of God. (See Judges 18:6, 1 Samuel 1:17, and 1 Samuel 20:42.) See also 2 Samuel 15:9 and 2 Kings 5:19.

Gospel writings show Jesus as having said these words only three times: to the woman in the present parable, accompanied by "your faith has saved you" (Luke 7:50); and to the hemorrhaging woman as he healed her, accompanied by "your faith has made you well" (Mark 5:34 and Luke 8:48).

In later New Testament writings, the jailer, releasing Paul, told him to go in peace. (See Acts 16:36.) James suggests the common phrase was empty if not accompanied by action: "If a brother or sister is naked and lacks daily food, and one of you says to them, 'Go in peace; keep warm and eat your fill,' and yet you do not supply their bodily needs, what is the good of that? So faith by itself, if it has no works, is dead" (James 2:15-17).

Mary

The devoted woman has no name in the present or any other version of the story in the Synoptic Gospels; however the writer of the Gospel of John identifies her: "Mary was the one who anointed the Lord with perfume and wiped his feet with her hair; her brother Lazarus was ill" (John 11:2).

Tears And Weeping

The first two passages of 44 that refer to "weep" exemplify two reasons for weeping. They were grief, as Hagar felt upon abandoning her son (Genesis 21:16) and being overcome with affection, as was Joseph when reunited with his brother Benjamin (Genesis 43:30). There are 52 references to "weeping" and 56 to "wept."

The folk of Bible times were an expressive, emotional lot. Note the volume of tears: "... drench you with my tears" (Isaiah 16:9); "a fountain of tears" (Jeremiah 9:10); tears that "stream down like a torrent day and night" (Lamentations 2:18); and of "rivers of tears" (Lamentations 3:48). The Psalmist also spoke of many tears: "... every night I flood my bed with tears; / I drench my couch with my weeping" (Psalm 6:6).

For the woman in the present story, this was such a time to weep. (See Ecclesiastes 3:4.) In contrast, the Psalmist, knowing that God is for him, sings, "You have kept count of my tossings; / *put my tears in your bottle. /* Are they not in your record?" (Psalm 56:8).

Jesus also took notice of the woman's tears. Perhaps he understood the private tears of a special relationship; however, the following words suggest that Jesus did not want to be the focus of public lament: When an uproar of weeping started as they led Jesus toward Golgotha, "Jesus turned to them and said, 'Daughters of Jerusalem, do not weep for me, but weep for yourselves and for your children'" (Luke 23:28).

The tears of another person moved Jesus to compassion. (See Luke 7:13.) When Jesus saw Mary weeping over Lazarus' death, he himself wept for his friend. (See John 11:35.) Yet he was not always sympathetic to tears. "When he had entered, he said to them, 'Why do you make a commotion and weep? The child is not dead but sleeping'" (Mark 5:39).

Touch (-ed, -es, -ing)

In Genesis 20:3-6, 2 Samuel 14:10, Esther 9:10 and 9:15, Proverbs 6:29, and 1 Corinthians 7:1, "touch" referred to intimate contact. In the present story, the host's choice of the word "touch" suggests further derision of Jesus' authority. See Luke 7:39.

Jesus had a healing touch. See Matthew 8:3, 8:15, 9:29, 17:7, and 20:34; Mark 1:41; and Luke 22:51. When hurting people heard that Jesus' touch had made others whole, they wanted to touch him. "And all in the crowd were trying to touch him, for power came out from him and healed all of them" (Luke 6:19). See also Matthew 9:21 and 14:36; Mark 3:10, 5:28, 6:56, 8:22, and 10:13; and Luke 18:15. Was there, beyond the healing touch, the other, universal yearning to making contact with the holy (Exodus 30:29)?

The laws in Leviticus take touching seriously. Touch contact was thought to transmit more than disease. Touch something holy to become holy. Touch what is unholy and become unholy. Touch something unclean and become unclean.

Laugh? Touch someone with cancer and become cancerous. Touch someone who is blind and you become blind. Negative or ill-intentioned touch makes one squirm or recoil. Positive touch draws two persons closer. Make touch contact, lay a hand on someone's shoulder, or shake the hands and something spiritual passes between you, a bond, a connecting of soul with soul.

4. Parallel Gospels

Faith

In the present parable, Jesus tells the woman, "Your faith has saved you; go in peace" (Luke 7:50). In the miracle of the hemorrhaging woman, Jesus told her, "Take heart, daughter, your faith has made you well" (Matthew 9:22). In Mark's version, "[Jesus] said to her, 'Daughter, your faith has made you well'" (Mark 5:34a). Mark adds, " 'Go in peace, and be healed of your disease' " (Mark 5:34b). Jesus told Bartimaeus, who was blind, " 'Go, your faith has made you well' " (Mark 10:52).

Woman With Alabaster Jar Of Ointment

Luke reveals neither that Jesus was at Bethany nor that Simon was a leper, as do Mark and Matthew. (See Mark 14:3 and Matthew 26:6.) Luke says only that "a woman in the city, who was a sinner" (Luke 7:37).

Luke mentions "sinner" twice (Luke 7:37 and 7:39b) and "sins" twice (Luke 7:48 and 7:49). Mark and Matthew say nothing about her being a sinner.

Mark says nothing about Simon's being a Pharisee. Luke not only mentions "Pharisee" four times, he also emphasizes the ongoing squabble that causes Jesus to tell the parable. Mark says only that "some were there who said to one another in anger ..." (Mark 14:4). In Matthew's telling, others at the table were the disciples. They were angry at the waste, suggesting the ointment could have been better used. (See Matthew 26:9.)

When these people scold her, Jesus tells them, somewhat abruptly, "Let her alone, why do you trouble her? She has performed a good service for me" (Mark 14:6a). In Matthew's telling, Jesus says, "Why do you trouble the woman? She has performed a good service for me" (Matthew 26:10).

In Luke's version, the Pharisee demeans Jesus' authority, saying, "If this man were a prophet ..." (Luke 7:39). Mark emphasized wondering why the "very costly ointment of nard" was "wasted in this way" (Mark 14:3 and 4). In Mark, the antagonist stresses that the ointment could have been sold and money given to the poor.

(See Mark 14:5.) Matthew stressed the disciples' anger, "Why this waste? For this ointment could have been sold for a large sum, and the money given to the poor" (Matthew 26:8). Luke speaks also of an alabaster jar of ointment (Luke 7:37) but neither Luke nor Matthew calls it nard or very costly. Matthew speaks of "an alabaster jar of very costly ointment" but not of nard. (See Matthew 26:7.)

Luke stresses the quality of love. He illustrates his point both with the woman's kindness and by telling the story of the two debtors. In Mark, Jesus foreshadows his death twice: "She has anointed my body beforehand for its burial" (Mark 14:8). Matthew records, "By pouring this ointment on my body she has prepared me for burial" (Matthew 26:12).

The second foreshadowing reads, "For you will always have the poor with you, and you can show kindness to them whenever you wish; but you will not always have me" (Mark 14:7). In Matthew's telling, Jesus says, "For you always have the poor with you, but you will not always have me" (Matthew 26:11). In Luke, Jesus suggests none of this; however, Luke uses the word "anoint" three times: "... [S]he continued kissing his feet and anointing them" (Luke 7:38b) and "You did not anoint my head with oil, but she has anointed my feet ..." (Luke 7:46). Use of this word hints at a special, devoted touching of the body. In keeping with Matthew's emphasis on Jesus' fulfillment of Hebrew Scripture, Matthew says the woman poured the oil on Jesus' head as he sat at the table. (See Matthew 26:7.)

A strong line in Mark's version is "She has done what she could" (Mark 14:8a), while a strong line in Luke's is "She has shown great love" (Luke 7:47b). In Matthew, a strong line is "She has performed a good service for me" (Matthew 26:10b).

Matthew and Mark conclude with this line: "Truly I tell you, wherever this good news is proclaimed in the whole world, what she has done will be told in remembrance of her" (Matthew 26:13). Mark uses "the good news." (See Mark 14:9.)

Parallel Story From John

The setting is also at Bethany. It was at the home of Lazarus rather than Simon. Martha served, and Mary anointed Jesus' feet with "a pound of costly perfume made of pure nard" (John 12:3) wiping them with her hair.

This later version contains several parenthetical and interpretive phrases. It emphasizes the coming events: It was six days before the Passover. Judas Iscariot "(the one who was about to betray him)" (John 12:4) scolded about the perfume. John says, "He said this not because he cared about the poor, but because he was a thief" (John 12:6). When Jesus told him to leave her alone, he said, "She bought it so that she might keep it for the day of my burial" (John 12:7b).

John says, "You always have the poor with you, but you do not always have me" (John 12:8). Matthew says, "For you," and "you will not always." See Matthew 26:11. Mark has the embellished statement: "For you always have the poor with you, and you can show kindness to them whenever you wish; but you will not always have me" (Mark 14:7).

5. Chat Room

Chat A
Elmer: The topic is love.

Joe: Love? Now, how do you figure that, Elmer?

Elmer: That's the only way I can understand it.

Joe: How *did* you fare with the creditor?

Elmer: He forgave my debt, Joe. Because of his faith in me, I get to start over.

Joe: He let mine go, too, but I figured it was slim enough he could just write it off.

Elmer: Forgiving a debt ten times the size of yours is unheard of in our work. I'll love that one forever. Do you want to know what he said as I left his place? He said, " 'Forgive us our debts.' I believe in a compassionate God."

Chat B
D: Could we talk about that day at the Pharisee's house?

M: It was ironic. The host did not even offer Jesus basic hospitality. In your world, you offer to take the coat or something to drink or direct them to the facilities. Here, people often walk great distances. Nothing feels better than to remove sandals and wash hot, dusty feet before anything else. Nothing.

I suppose that's what set off the tears. That blasted Pharisee. When I saw that Jesus' feet had no attention, I must tell you, I surprised myself. I had not planned to cry. I didn't say a word. I just started weeping. All my unspoken words of a lifetime came pouring out in tears. I had no towel. I used what I had. My hair fell onto his precious, burning feet.

D: Weeping seems to stop then flow again from a seemingly endless supply. Your tears fell before you even began to anoint Jesus.

M: The more I listened to that Pharisee, the more they fell — from rage, from my own grief, the thought of his having to waste his time with being taunted. I know what it is like to be taunted. By the time I remembered the anointing oil, a devotion that I did not know I had came tumbling out unrestrained in kisses, holy kisses of the feet of a holy one.

He was not even gone, yet my grieving was as keen as if he had died. Without really understanding, I anointed his feet with oil made holy by a love he awakened in me like none other. Jesus was a good person. I saw the grief of human suffering he quieted with his healing. I followed his journey from a distance. I stayed in the background but heard about his dedication to the people. Even though I was of ill-chosen repute with a long list of sinning, I knew about Jesus.

D: He knew about you.

M: He knew all about me without my having said a word. I felt acceptable in his presence. He did not push me away. I spoke no words. I did not interfere. He accepted my gift. I was his servant, washing his feet and anointing him, an anointing surely as holy as if with consecrating oil of the temple poured over his head. He knew. That's why he told Simon a thing or two in my defense.

Did you hear his lovely "therefore" and "hence"? Did you hear him forgive me? Did you hear him tell me to go in peace?

D: You showed great love.

M: To the worst among us, God shows great love, compassion, and forgiveness.

---

1. See "Alabaster" in George A. Buttrick, Ed. *The Interpreter's Dictionary of the Bible, V. A-D* (Nashville: Abingdon Press, 1962) and <www.encyclopedia.com>.

Parable 6

The Good Samaritan

Luke 10:25-37

---

1. Text

Just then a lawyer stood up to test Jesus. "Teacher," he said, "what must I do to inherit eternal life?" [26] He said to him, "What is written in the law? What do you read there?" [27] He answered, "You shall love the Lord your God with all your heart, and with all your soul, and with all your strength, and with all your mind; and your neighbor as yourself." [28] And he said to him, "You have given the right answer; do this, and you will live."

[29] But wanting to justify himself, he asked Jesus, "And who is my neighbor?" [30] Jesus replied, "A man was going down from Jerusalem to Jericho, and fell into the hands of robbers, who stripped him, beat him, and went away, leaving him half dead. [31] Now by chance a priest was going down that road; and when he saw him, he passed by on the other side. [32] So likewise a Levite, when he came to the place and saw him, passed by on the other side. [33] But a Samaritan while traveling came near him; and when he saw him, he was moved with pity. [34] He went to him and bandaged his wounds, having poured oil and wine on them. Then he put him on his own animal, brought him to an inn, and took care of him. [35] The next day he took out two denarii, gave them to the innkeeper, and said, 'Take care of him; and when I come back, I will repay you whatever more you spend.' [36] Which of these three, do you think, was a

neighbor to the man who fell into the hands of the rob-
bers?" [37] He said, "The one who showed him mercy."
Jesus said to him, "Go and do likewise."

2. What's Happening?

First Point Of Action

Testing Jesus, a lawyer asks what he must do to inherit eternal life. Jesus returns his query with his own, asking for his interpretation of the law. The lawyer answers with the Mosaic "love God" formula. Jesus applauds him adding the ending of the Deuteronomic formula, "in order that you may live."

Second Point Of Action

Continuing his questioning, the lawyer asks who his neighbor is and Jesus tells the parable.

Third Point Of Action

Robbers attacked a man traveling from Jerusalem to Jericho. They stripped and beat him, leaving him for dead.

Fourth Point Of Action

A priest passed him by on the other side of the road.

Fifth Point Of Action

A Levite passed him by on the other side of the road.

Sixth Point Of Action

A Samaritan came by and, moved with compassion, cleaned and bound his wounds.

Seventh Point Of Action

He put the wounded man on his animal, took him to an inn, and cared for him.

Eighth Point Of Action

Next day, he paid the innkeeper two denarii to continue his care and said he would pay for any additional costs when he returned.

Ninth Point Of Action

In his third conversation with the lawyer, Jesus asks which of the three travelers acted as a neighbor to the injured man. The lawyer said it was the one who showed him mercy. Jesus told him to go do likewise.

3. Spade Work

Eternal Life

When the lawyer asked Jesus what he must do to inherit eternal life, Jesus told him the parable of The Good Samaritan. When a ruler asked Jesus what he must do to inherit eternal life, Jesus told him to sell all of his possessions. (See Luke 10:25 and 18:18ff. See also Matthew 19:16 and 19:29-30 and Mark 10:17-22.)

Followers also must leave house and family. (See Luke 18:29-30 and Mark 10:29-30.) Those who ignore the hungry, thirsty, stranger, naked, sick, or in prison "will go away into eternal punishment, but the righteous into eternal life" (Matthew 25:44-46).

The Gospel of John contains fifteen references to "eternal life," beginning with the most familiar: "And just as Moses lifted up the serpent in the wilderness, so must the Son of Man be lifted up, that whoever believes in him may have eternal life. For God so loved the world that he gave his only Son, so that everyone who believes in him may not perish but may have eternal life" (John 3:14-16).

The prerequisite to eternal life for "whoever" and "anyone" is belief in the Son (John 3:36, 5:24, 5:39-40, 6:40, and 6:47); the water Christ gives will bring eternal life (John 4:14); and those who eat Christ's flesh and drink his blood (John 6:54).

Those who disobey the Son will not see eternal life. (See John 3:36.) "Those who love their life lose it, and those who hate their life in this world will keep it for eternal life" (John 12:25). "... [S]ince you have given him authority over all people, to give eternal life to all whom you have given him. And this is eternal life, that they may know you, the only true God, and Jesus Christ whom you have sent" (John 17:2-3).

Mercy

"Mercy" is a whole Bible word, occurring 105 times with twenty occasions in the New Testament. "Merciful" appears 24 times. God is "merciful and gracious" (see Exodus 34:6; 2 Chronicles 30:9; Nehemiah 9:17 and 31; Psalm 86:15, 103:8, 111:4, 112:4, 116:5, and 145:8; Joel 2:13; and Jonah 4:2. Several of these verses include a formula seen in Nehemiah 9:17, of "the Lord, your God, for he is gracious and merciful, slow to anger, and abounding in steadfast love").

Can the mercy of a faithful God have a capricious element? "[God told Moses], 'I will make all my goodness pass before you, and will proclaim before you the name, "The Lord"; and I will be gracious to whom I will be gracious, and will show mercy on whom I will show mercy' " (Exodus 33:19). This passage suggests that God does not want to be the object of our manipulation.

When Paul paraphrased this passage, he added the following observation: "So it depends not on human will or exertion, but on God who shows mercy" (Romans 9:15-16). So is this why in the most dire circumstances, we leave reaching out to people and send our plea for help directly to God?

Numerous passages refer to the specially constructed "mercy seat" where God arranged to meet with Moses. See Exodus 25:13-22, 26:34, 30:6, 31:7, 35:12, 37:6-9, and 39:35; Leviticus 16:2 and 16:13-15; Numbers 7:89; 1 Chronicles 28:11; and Hebrews 9:5.

The following two passages offer particular comfort: "Because the Lord your God is a merciful God, he will neither abandon you nor destroy you; he will not forget the covenant with your ancestors that he swore to them" (Deuteronomy 4:31) and "Be merciful to me, O God, be merciful to me, / for in you my soul takes refuge; / in the shadow of your wings I will take refuge, / until the destroying storms pass by" (Psalm 57:1). Other descriptions of God as merciful are found in Genesis 19:16, Deuteronomy 4:31, and Jeremiah 3:12.

The mercy of God is intertwined with justice: "Great is your mercy, O Lord; / give me life according to your justice" (Psalm 119:156) and "Therefore the Lord waits to be gracious to you; / therefore he will rise up to show mercy to you. / For the Lord is a

God of justice; / blessed are all those who wait for him" (Isaiah 30:18).

Mercy has to do with God's keeping us safe as well as saving us: "Surely goodness and mercy shall follow me / all the days of my life, / and I shall dwell in the house of the Lord / my whole life long" (Psalm 23:6) and "Do not, O Lord, withhold / your mercy from me; / let your steadfast love and your faithfulness / keep me safe forever" (Psalm 40:10).

Who are the recipients of mercy? "His mercy is for those who fear him from generation to generation" (Luke 1:50).

The plea for mercy requires persistence: "As the eyes of servants / look to the hand of their master, / as the eyes of a maid to the hand of her mistress, / so our eyes look to the Lord our God, / until he has mercy upon us" (Psalm 123:2); "Have mercy upon us, O Lord, have mercy upon us, / for we have had more than enough of contempt" (Psalm 123:3); and "But the tax collector, standing far off, would not even look up to heaven, but was beating his breast and saying, 'God, be merciful to me, a sinner!' " (Luke 18:13).

In the miracle stories, the plea of the hurting or their advocates was "Lord, have mercy on me" (see Matthew 9:27, 15:22, 17:15, and 20:30; Mark 10:47; Luke 16:24, 17:13, and 18:38). Jesus responds to the words of the prophet, Hosea: "For I desire steadfast love and not sacrifice, the knowledge of God rather than burnt offerings" (Hosea 6:6). He tells the Pharisees to "[g]o and learn what this means, 'I desire mercy, not sacrifice.' For I have come to call not the righteous but sinners" (Matthew 9:13). (See also Matthew 12:7.)

Not only are we recipients of mercy, we are to show mercy to others: "Thus says the Lord of hosts: Render true judgments, show kindness and mercy to one another" (Zechariah 7:9) and "Be merciful, just as your Father is merciful" (Luke 6:36).

Jesus calls justice, mercy, and faith the "weightier matters of the law." (See Matthew 23:23.) He counsels the practice of mercy: "Should you not have had mercy on your fellow slave, as I had mercy on you?" (Matthew 18:33) and "Blessed are the merciful, for they will receive mercy" (Matthew 5:7).

Neighbor

Fifty of the 66 references to "neighbor" are found in the Hebrew Scripture. Ten are in the Synoptic Gospels. Six of the 44 references to "neighbors" are in the Synoptic Gospels.

Who is your neighbor? A neighbor is one who lives near or next to another, a person, place, or thing adjacent to or located near another, a fellow human being, a near dweller, now even one whom one does not know. What about the cyber-neighbor who lives miles away and yet is close in spirit?

Who is your neighbor? "If there is among you anyone in need, a member of your community in any of your towns within the land that the Lord your God is giving you, do not be hard-hearted or tight-fisted toward your needy neighbor" (Deuteronomy 15:7). "Since there will never cease to be some in need on the earth, I therefore command you, 'Open your hand to the poor and needy neighbor in your land' " (Deuteronomy 15:11).

Two of the Ten Commandments speak of how to treat one's neighbor: "You shall not bear false witness against your neighbor" (Exodus 20:16) and "You shall not covet your neighbor's house; you shall not covet your neighbor's wife, or male or female slave, or ox, or donkey, or anything that belongs to your neighbor" (Exodus 20:17).

According to Deuteronomic law, as a neighbor, you "may not withhold your help. You shall not see your neighbor's donkey or ox fallen on the road and ignore it; you shall help to lift it up" (Deuteronomy 22:3b-4). "And if your neighbor cries out to me, I will listen, for I am compassionate" (Exodus 22:27). "You shall not defraud your neighbor" (Leviticus 19:13a). "[W]ith justice you shall judge your neighbor" (Leviticus 19:15c). "You shall not take vengeance or bear a grudge against any of your people, but you shall love your neighbor as yourself: I am the Lord" (Leviticus 19:18).

There is the good neighbor code; then there is everyday reality. The closer one lives to a neighbor, the more difficult it may be to relate, let alone love that neighbor. "Return sevenfold into the bosom of our neighbors the taunts with which they taunted you, O Lord!" (Psalm 79:12). "The poor are disliked even by their neighbors, but the rich have many friends. Those who despise their neighbors are sinners, but happy are those who are kind to the poor" (Proverbs 14:20-21). "They all speak friendly words to their neighbors, but inwardly are planning to lay an ambush" (Jeremiah 9:8). See also Proverbs 3:29, Proverbs 27:14, and Jeremiah 9:4.

The reality code suggests when trouble happens across the street with the neighbors, that you indulge your curiosity and look between the blinds with your lights off but avoid running full speed to their assistance. Give them space; you would not want to intrude. Call 911 anonymously: "My friends and companions stand aloof from my affliction, and my neighbors stand far off" (Psalm 38:11).

One cannot have the same unattended problem as a neighbor and expect to be of help. "Or how can you say to your neighbor, 'Let me take the speck out of your eye,' while the log is in your own eye?" (Matthew 7:4 and Luke 6:42).

On being a good neighbor, follow the basic Golden Rule of the human family: "In everything do to others as you would have them do to you; for this is the law and the prophets" (Matthew 7:12 and Luke 6:31). "Honor your father and mother; also, You shall love your neighbor as yourself" (Matthew 19:19). See also Matthew 5:43, Matthew 22:39, Mark 12:31, and Luke 10:27. Loving one's neighbor as oneself as well as loving God "is much more important than all whole burnt offerings and sacrifices" (Mark 12:33).

"[Jesus] said also to the one who had invited him, 'When you give a luncheon or a dinner, do not invite your friends or your brothers or your relatives or rich neighbors, in case they may invite you in return, and you would be repaid' " (Luke 14:12). While Jesus was making a different point here, why not invite them all, both those who can repay and those who cannot? It might improve things in your neighborhood.

All is not dismal regarding neighbors. The woman who found her lost coin and the shepherd who found his lost sheep appreciate their neighbors enough to call them over to rejoice with them and to celebrate their good fortune. (See Lost And Found, Parable 13, Cycle C, Luke 15:1-10.)

When Naomi gave birth to her son in a strange country, the women of the neighborhood gathered around and took them both under their wing: "[They] gave him a name, saying, 'A son has been born to Naomi.' They named him Obed; he became the father of Jesse, the father of David" (Ruth 4:17). Good neighboring.

Samaritan

All six biblical references to "Samaritan" are found in the Gospels. In the story, The Ten Lepers, the one among the ten persons with leprosy who returned to thank Jesus after he was healed was a Samaritan. Luke notes this as an afterthought: "And he was a Samaritan" (Luke 17:16). In Luke 17:18, he referred to the man as a foreigner.

In The Good Samaritan Story, the man was traveling from Jerusalem down to Jericho. In The Ten Lepers, Jesus went through the region to a village between Samaria and Galilee on the way to Jerusalem. (See Luke 17:11.) In The Good Samaritan, two of the three potential neighbors kept their distance on the other side of the road. In The Ten Lepers, the lepers approached Jesus but kept their distance from him. Did the injured man have a chance to thank the Samaritan? In The Ten Lepers, all had a chance but only one returned to do so.

On the way from Judea to Galilee, Jesus had to pass through the territory of Samaria. At the Samaritan city of Sychar, he met the Samaritan woman at the well. (See John 4:5-26.) In addition to having a geography, the Samaritans were a religious community. While some of their practices were similar to those of the Hebrews, others were closer to Islam.

The traditional hostility between Jews and Samaritans remained alive. When Jesus asked the woman for a drink of water, it was she who questioned him because, parenthetically in the text, "Jews do not share things in common with Samaritans" (John 4:9b). The Jews considered the Samaritans heathens. The Samaritans saw themselves as repatriated exiles of Israel.[1]

4. Parallel Scripture

Heart, Soul, and Strength

Ten biblical passages relate to the Two Commandments spoken by Christ, "You shall love the Lord your God with all your heart, and with all your soul, and with all your strength, and with all your mind; and your neighbor as yourself" (Luke 10:27).

Four passages are from Deuteronomy. "With all your strength" and "your neighbor as yourself" are absent in Deuteronomy 6:5 and 10:12. Rather than Luke's "with all your mind," Deuteronomy 6:5 reads "with all your might." Deuteronomy 10:12 contains neither "mind" nor "might."

Unlike the Lukan passage and the earlier reference from Deuteronomy that begin, "You shall love the Lord your God with," Deuteronomy 10:12 prefaces the dictum with "Only to fear the Lord your God, to walk in all his ways, to love him" and then "to serve the Lord your God with all your heart and with all your soul."

The Deuteronomy 13:3 passage speaks of God's testing the priestly tribe of Levi "to know whether you indeed love the Lord your God with all your heart and soul." The Deuteronomy 30:6 passage refers to loving God "with all your heart and with all your soul, in order that you may live."

In 1 Kings 8:23 and 2 Chronicles 6:14, God's reward for "your servants who walk before you with all their heart" is keeping God's covenant and steadfast love. The Joshua reference summarizes the commandment from Moses, concluding with the heart/soul formula: "to love the Lord your God, to walk in all his ways, to keep his commandments, and to hold fast to him, and to serve him with all your heart and with all your soul" (Joshua 22:5). He uses "serve," as it appears in Deuteronomy 10:12.

In the Synoptic Gospels, Mark's parallel more closely resembles that of Luke. Mark puts the "with all your mind" phrase before "with all your strength." Matthew uses heart, soul, and mind but omits strength. (See Matthew 22:37.) Mark and Matthew omit "and your neighbor as yourself," which is integral to the present parable. (See Mark 12:30.)

That You May Live

"And he said to him, 'You have given the right answer; do this, and you will live'" (Luke 10:28). This phrase that completes the Two Commandments suggests both physical survival with a thriving longevity (see Deuteronomy 5:33, 8:1, and 16:20) and a vibrant quality of the soul. (See the Deuteronomic "Choose life" passage from Deuteronomy 30:19-20.) In this passage, the qualifiers of choosing life "so that you and your descendants may live," include "loving the Lord your God, obeying him, and holding fast to him" (Deuteronomy 30:19-20). The choice to connect to God and be faithful to God is a prerequisite of life. See Isaiah 55:3 and Amos 5:14.

5. Chat Room

A: Where is your mercy seat? Where do you go to sit and wait for God? What special place have you built in your heart to go to and meet God? Where does God come to you?

B: How do you offer the mercy seat to a stranger? How do you bring God? Where do you go to show God's mercy? How do you love your neighbor as yourself?

A: Who is my neighbor? George Aamoth, Nana Kwuku Danso, Julie M. Geis.[2]

B: Forgetting inconvenience to themselves, good Samaritans allow compassion to move them. Samaritans bypass questions of citizenship, social security number, and insurance to become brothers or sisters to someone's wife or husband, someone's child, someone's father or mother, someone's sister or brother.

A: Who is my neighbor? Mon Gjonbalaj, Taizo Ishikawa, Mary Jones.

B: The Samaritan cares not if the injured one is from Ghana, India, Queens, or Japan. The Samaritan cares not if the injured one is brown or lesbian or blind. The Samaritan wants to find and tend.

A: Who is my neighbor? Shashi Kadabah, Jong-min Lee, Robert M. Levine.

B: The Samaritan cares not if the injured one worships the same God as the Samaritan, holds the same beliefs, or professes no belief at all. The Samaritan hears only the cry of a member of the human family.

A: Who is my neighbor? Brian Monaghan, Hardai Parbhu, Khalid Shahid.

B: Do you hear the voice of the hurting one call out to God in the soul when unable to use a spoken voice? When it seems too late, the savior of the injured one perceives beyond body, connecting soul with soul. The Samaritan hears the wordless call of those who suffer injustice and initiates a conversation of hope.

A: Who is my neighbor? John Sherry, Roshan/Khami Singh, Norbert Szurkowski.

B: When the hurt one cannot be fixed, God's portable mercy enters the dust and smoke. The pit becomes God's mercy seat. The holiness of God seeps through the crevices, finding the dust and bringing the mercy of the one who will be with us everywhere and always.

A: Who is my neighbor? Malissa White, Kevin Yokum, Igor Zukelman.

---

1. For further comparison of their religious practices, see "Samaritans, Affinities With Islam" and "Karaite Affinities" in George A. Buttrick, Ed., *The Interpreter's Dictionary Of The Bible, Volume 4* (Nashville: Abingdon Press, 1962).

2. The men and women named here are among the victims of the September 11, 2001, Twin Towers attack.

Parable 7

A Midnight Friend

Luke 11:1-13

---

1. Text

He was praying in a certain place, and after he had finished, one of his disciples said to him, "Lord, teach us to pray, as John taught his disciples." [2] He said to them, "When you pray, say: Father, hallowed be your name. Your kingdom come. [3] Give us each day our daily bread. [4] And forgive us our sins, for we ourselves forgive everyone indebted to us. And do not bring us to the time of trial."

[5] And he said to them, "Suppose one of you has a friend, and you go to him at midnight and say to him, 'Friend, lend me three loaves of bread; [6] for a friend of mine has arrived, and I have nothing to set before him.' [7] And he answers from within, 'Do not bother me; the door has already been locked, and my children are with me in bed; I cannot get up and give you anything.' [8] I tell you, even though he will not get up and give him anything because he is his friend, at least because of his persistence he will get up and give him whatever he needs.

[9] "So I say to you, Ask, and it will be given you; search, and you will find; knock, and the door will be opened for you. [10] For everyone who asks receives, and everyone who searches finds, and for everyone who knocks, the door will be opened. [11] Is there anyone among you who, if your child asks for a fish, will give a

snake instead of a fish? [12] Or if the child asks for an egg, will give a scorpion? [13] If you then, who are evil, know how to give good gifts to your children, how much more will the heavenly Father give the Holy Spirit to those who ask him!"

2. What's Happening?

First Point Of Action

Jesus responds to the request of a disciple to teach the disciples to pray as John taught his disciples by teaching them the Prayer of our Savior.

Second Point Of Action

Jesus tells the present parable. A person to whose house a friend has arrived unexpectedly at midnight goes to the house of another friend at midnight and asks him for three loaves of bread as he has nothing in his own house with which to show hospitality.

Third Point Of Action

At first the friend refuses. He has already locked his door for the night and is settled into bed with his family.

Fourth Point Of Action

The asking person persists. Jesus says the friend finally gets up and gives him what he needs not because of their friendship but because of his persistence.

Fifth Point Of Action

Jesus speaks the familiar trilogy of sayings: Ask, and it will be given you. Search, and you will find. Knock, and the door will be opened for you.

Sixth Point Of Action

Jesus adds the mini-parable about the human parent, albeit with human shortcomings, who gives to the child who asks not something that will harm that child but gives only good gifts.

Seventh Point Of Action

Jesus makes the analogy between the care of the flawed human parent and the generosity of God as a spiritual parent.

3. Spadework

Ask/Receive

For what do we ask? What were the biblical people asking of God? How did God respond to their asking?

"[A]nd we receive from him whatever we ask, because we obey his commandments and do what pleases him" (1 John 3:22). God found pleasure in Solomon's request also. When God said to him, "Ask what I should give you," Solomon said, "Give your servant therefore an understanding mind to govern your people, able to discern between good and evil; for who can govern this your great people?"

In turn, "God said to [Solomon], 'Because you have asked this, and have not asked for yourself long life or riches, or for the life of your enemies, but have asked for yourself understanding to discern what is right, I now do according to your word. Indeed I give you a wise and discerning mind; no one like you has been before you and no one like you shall arise after you. I give you also what you have not asked, both riches and honor all your life; no other king shall compare with you' " (from 1 Kings 3:5-13). See also 2 Chronicles 1:7.

Were the Psalmist's questions, then, the wrong questions? Hoping for a word from God, the Psalmist asks, "When will you comfort me?" and "How long must your servant endure?" and "When will you judge those who persecute me?" See Psalm 119:81-84.

What type of asking is best? Zechariah suggests that our prayers be timely: "Ask rain from the Lord in the season of the spring rain" (Zechariah 10:1). We may ask for the wrong things: "You ask and do not receive, because you ask wrongly, in order to spend what you get on your pleasures" (James 4:3). "And he sighed deeply in his spirit and said, 'Why does this generation ask for a sign? Truly I tell you, no sign will be given to this generation' " (Mark 8:12).

God invites our asking: "I will tell of the decree of the Lord: / He said to me, 'You are my son; / today I have begotten you. / Ask of me, and I will make the nations your heritage, / and the ends of the earth your possession' " (Psalm 2:7-8).

Can one imagine even God's frustration and sense of helplessness when God stands ready for being approached and no one comes? We miss-communicate even with God. After much had happened, Isaiah says to God, "After all this, will you restrain yourself, O Lord? Will you keep silent, and punish us so severely?" (Isaiah 64:12).

God answers Isaiah: "I was ready to be sought out by those who did not ask, to be found by those who did not seek me. I said, 'Here I am, here I am,' to a nation that did not call on my name. I held out my hands all day long to a rebellious people, who walk in a way that is not good, following their own devices" (Isaiah 65:1-2).

When God asked Ahaz to ask a sign of God, Ahaz refused, saying, "I will not ask, and I will not put the Lord to the test" (Isaiah 7:12). Whereupon, Isaiah, chiding Ahaz for wearying God with his messing around, said the Lord himself would *give* him a sign without his asking. (See Isaiah 7:14.)

As with many of our prayers, we initially plan to ask for "two things" then ask for more: "Two things I ask of you; do not deny them to me before I die: Remove far from me falsehood and lying; give me neither poverty nor riches; feed me with the food that I need" (Proverbs 30:7-8). The Proverb writer gains in boldness, stomping his foot with this ultimatum: "or I shall be full, and deny you, and say, 'Who is the Lord?' or I shall be poor, and steal, and profane the name of my God" (Proverbs 30:9).

The following Matthean passage is the benchmark on communication with God: "When you are praying, do not heap up empty phrases as the Gentiles do; for they think that they will be heard because of their many words. Do not be like them, for your Father knows what you need before you ask him" (Matthew 6:7-8). Before we even ask, God anticipates our needs.

Paul speaks to the wordless yearning that is itself prayer: "But if we hope for what we do not see, we wait for it with patience. Likewise the Spirit helps us in our weakness; for we do not know how to pray as we ought, but that very Spirit intercedes with sighs too deep for words. And God, who searches the heart, knows what is the mind of the Spirit, because the Spirit intercedes for the saints according to the will of God" (Romans 8:24-28).

Friend (Friendship)

Consider in this parable that the friend did not go to a relative for the bread. With some things, one dares not approach relatives. Only a friend will do. Might a relative judge, ridicule, scorn, or say, "Absolutely not. You can wait until morning"? Relatives are too risky. A friend is nearby but not as close as a relative. One can trust a good friend even with one's foolishness. One certainly can count on a friend during a crisis: "Do not forsake your friend or the friend of your parent; do not go to the house of your kindred in the day of your calamity. Better is a neighbor who is nearby than kindred who are far away" (Proverbs 27:10).

The code of Middle Eastern hospitality demands kindness in welcoming guests and strangers as well as friends. So also was the hospitality of those on the Great Plain. Folk traveling long distances across the mid-section of our country once needed to stay awhile to revive from the journey. Food was necessary for survival and for fortification for the continuation of the journey. Shelter was a necessity to protect travelers both from the elements and from wildlife. However, beyond the necessity of hospitality lies the friendship of being a neighbor.

Friendship requires generosity of spirit. "If there is among you anyone in need, a member of your community in any of your towns within the land that the Lord your God is giving you, do not be hard-hearted or tight-fisted toward your needy neighbor. You should rather open your hand, willingly lending enough to meet the need, whatever it may be" (Deuteronomy 15:7-8).

What is friendship about? "Some friends play at friendship but *a true friend sticks closer than one's nearest kin*" (Proverbs 18:24). Whereas relatives are "born to share adversity," according to Proverbs 17:17, "a friend loves at all times." Friends refrain from withholding kindness. See Job 6:14. David went out to meet [Benjaminites and Judahites who came to him] and said to them, "If you have come to me in friendship, to help me, then my heart will be knit to you" (1 Chronicles 12:17).

From among the six biblical references to "friendship" and the fifty references to "friend," one can glean several characteristics of God's friendship and our friendship with God: "Thus the Lord used *to speak* to Moses *face to face*, as one speaks to a friend" (Exodus 33:11a). "The friendship of the Lord is for those who fear him, / and he makes his covenant known to them" (Psalm 25:14). "Thus the scripture was fulfilled that says, 'Abraham believed God, and it was reckoned to him as *righteousness*,' and he was called *the friend of God*" (James 2:23). Christ was "a friend of tax collectors and sinners" (Luke 7:34).

Christ addressed a unique collection of acquaintances as "friend" at other singular moments in his ministry. When Judas betrayed Jesus with a kiss, "Jesus said to him, '*Friend,* do what you are here to do'" (Matthew 26:50a). In Luke 5:20, when Jesus saw the faith of the friends of the paralyzed man whom they let down through the roof, Jesus said to the stranger, "*Friend,* your sins are forgiven you." See also Luke 12:14 and 14:10.

Knock/Open

Not to everyone who knocks is the door opened: "When once the owner of the house has got up and shut the door, and you begin to stand outside and to knock at the door, saying, 'Lord, open to us,' then in reply he will say to you, 'I do not know where you come from'" (Luke 13:25).

The door must be open or opened before one can enter through it. "Open to me the gates of righteousness, / that I may enter through them / and give thanks to the Lord" (Psalm 118:19). Consider how we are to respond to the knock that comes on our door: "[T]he stranger has not lodged in the street; I have opened my doors to the traveler" (Job 31:32). "[B]e like those who are waiting for their master to return from the wedding banquet, so that they may open the door for him as soon as he comes and knocks" (Luke 12:36).

Are we ever to reject the person who comes to our door? "When once the owner of the house has got up and shut the door, and you begin to stand outside and to knock at the door, saying, 'Lord, open to us,' then in reply he will say to you, 'I do not know where you come from' " (Luke 13:25).

"Listen! I am standing at the door, knocking; if you hear my voice and open the door, I will come in to you and eat with you, and you with me" (Revelation 3:20). God wants us to be as prompt to open this door as those who waited for their master to return from the wedding banquet. (See Luke 12:36.)

God is a hospitable God who opens many doors for us unasked. For those who obey God, this generous God will "open for you a rich storehouse, the heavens, to give the rain of your land in its season and to bless all your undertakings" (Deuteronomy 28:12a). See Acts 14:27, 1 Corinthians 16:8-9, and Psalm 145:16.

Is it possible that, if we observe closely, we will notice that the door has been ajar all along? "I know your works. Look, I have set before you an open door, which no one is able to shut" (Revelation 3:8a).

Our Father

Christ tells us we are to address God as one who is as close to us and as caring for us as a parent. Isaiah gives further meaning to this closeness with God. As a parent, God stands ready to save or redeem us: "[Y]ou, O Lord, are our father; our Redeemer from of old is your name" (Isaiah 63:16b). "Therefore the Lord waits to be gracious to you; therefore he will rise up to show mercy to you" (Isaiah 30:18a).

As a parent, God is active creator and shaper, one who influences our being: "Yet, O Lord, you are our Father; we are the clay, and you are our potter; we are all the work of your hand" (Isaiah 64:8). "The Lord is just in all his ways, / and kind in all his doings. / The Lord is near to all who call on him, / to all who call on him in truth" (Psalm 145:17-18).

The present parable is the first of three in this cycle that address prayer. (See also Cycle C, Parable 17, The Uncaring Judge, and Cycle C, Parable 18, Two Men At Prayer.)

Seek/Find

Benchmark passages for the seek/find relationship we hold with God include the following: "I sought the Lord, and he answered me, / and delivered me from all my fears" (Psalm 34:4) and "When you search for me, you will find me; if you seek me with all your heart" (Jeremiah 29:13). See also Deuteronomy 4:29.

While we seek God, and even when we do not seek God, God is searching us: "You search out my path and my lying down, / and are acquainted with all my ways" (Psalm 139:3) and "For the Son of Man came to seek out and to save the lost" (Luke 19:10).

The Chronicles' historian suggests that active and persistent seeking will be fruitful: "Glory in his holy name; let the hearts of those who seek the Lord rejoice. Seek the Lord and his strength, seek his presence continually" (1 Chronicles 16:10-11). See also Psalm 105:3-4.

We underestimate the proximity of God through those difficult times that draw us toward feelings of abandonment or isolation. We might slip then into wondering if God has gone "where we cannot come." "Jesus then said, 'I will be with you a little while longer, and then I am going to him who sent me. You will search for me, but you will not find me; and where I am, you cannot come'" (John 7:33-34), and "With their flocks and herds they shall go to seek the Lord, but they will not find him; he has withdrawn from them" (Hosea 5:6).

Most needing to seek God's presence are also vulnerable to a lack of trust and of the faith that God still is present. God is still present and as immediate as the Psalmist's use of the present tense, "you discern": "O Lord, you have searched me and known me. / You know when I sit down and when I rise up; / you discern my thoughts from far away" (Psalm 139:1-2).

"And you, my son Solomon, know the God of your father, and serve him with single mind and willing heart; for the Lord searches every mind, and understands every plan and thought. If you seek him, he will be found by you; but if you forsake him, he will abandon you forever" (1 Chronicles 28:9). See also Jeremiah 17:10.

God answers our call: "[B]ut when in their distress [Israel] turned to the Lord, the God of Israel, and sought him, he was found by them" (2 Chronicles 15:4). "[T]hose who seek the Lord lack no good thing" (Psalm 34:10b).

4. Parallel Scripture

This parable is unique to the New Testament. Consider the following Ask, Seek, and Knock passages:

Ask, And You Shall Receive
"So I tell you, whatever you ask for *in prayer, believe* that you have received it, and it will be yours" (Mark 11:24).

"Whatever you ask for *in prayer with faith*, you will receive" (Matthew 21:22).

"On that day you will ask nothing of me. Very truly, I tell you, if you ask anything of the Father *in my name*, he will give it to you. Until now you have not asked for anything in my name. Ask and you will receive, *so that* your joy may be complete" (John 16:23-24).

"You did not choose me but *I chose you*. And I appointed you to go and bear fruit, fruit that will last, so that the Father will give you whatever you ask him in my name" (John 15:16).

"*If you abide in me, and my words abide in you*, ask for whatever you wish, and it will be done for you" (John 15:7).

After the Lukan preface of "So I say to you," Luke mirrors the Matthew 7:7 parallel of the ask-seek-knock sayings.

5. Chat Room

Charles: Why did you go to your friend at midnight of all times? And did you have to have three loaves of bread?

Reuben: Isn't that always when the emergencies occur? I had no choice. I did not expect my friend's arrival. He was exhausted, hungry. He had missed the evening meal. You know that is the main meal. I had to feed him plenty to be gracious, to honor him. He is my friend. I could not send him away either empty-of-stomach or empty-handed. I would have done the same had my trusted friend come to my own door at midnight.

Charles: You know that your friend needed some convincing to open his door.

Reuben: I do, but I also know that my friend is a friend. If I could rouse him enough, wake him up enough, he would come to the door. I owe him one.

Charles: How far is too far too push in friendship? At some point I would not get out of bed for anyone. Are you online yet, Jeanne?

Jeanne: I'm back. I been wondering if that breadth of hospitality holds true with prayer. Reuben's generosity suggests to me that God's relationship to us also is one of hospitality. I think of praying as addressing a trusted friend upon whom I can count.

Charles: So what is prayer? Why do we persist in praying to God? Can we pray too much and drive God away?

Jeanne: Sometimes prayer is active on my part, but mostly prayer comes to me. Sometimes I am intentional about praying, but mostly it catches me unawares. As my thoughts turn to pondering, I find myself addressing them to God, including God as listener. I feel welcome before God. I do not have to censor my words but speak freely.

Charles: For me, prayer is as much action and relating with others as speaking words. When I treat a friend or even a stranger in a way consistent with my faith, God is present. That is prayer. I'm better at living a prayer than shaping the words. I get a lot of things sorted out as I go about the routine chores of the day. In that time, I may not have addressed God in the form of a prayer, yet I have been communicating with God the entire time.

Jeanne: The way we ask, seek, and knock is not as important as that we persist in asking, seeking, and knocking because we sense that we are welcome to do so. We have to have someone to talk to, soul to soul, with or without words. Otherwise, the struggle is too lonely. The challenge is too likely to overwhelm. The job of peace-making is too great.

Charles: How are we to pray? What if the Prayer of our Savior were the only prayer to which we gave words? It was, after all, Christ's answer to the disciple who asked him to teach the disciples how to pray. It has, after all, been the communal prayer of the people at weekly worship for a long time.

Jeanne: When you think about it, all of the basics are there. We address God as one might speak to a trusted and revered parent. Our hope is for the realm of God to be a reality. Despite our supposed independence, we are interdependent and concerned about physical needs. We fall short in our relationships to God and those with each other. We know about fear. It is all there in this prayer.

Charles: Why do we persist in praying to God in the first place? After a while I get to thinking that God is causing all the turmoil of the human family. If God is not in charge, if God cannot do anything about the messes in our world, then why do we persist in praying to God?

Jeanne: I think of prayer as our determination not to be undone by fear, terror, or the waiting for the unknown to happen. Perhaps the prayer is the persistence. Perhaps prayer is itself the expression of hope. Perhaps praying is our opening the door to empower God's hospitality to happen.

Charles: Perhaps.

Parable 8

The Rich Fool

Luke 12:13-21

---

1. Text

> *Someone in the crowd said to him, "Teacher, tell my brother to divide the family inheritance with me." [14] But he said to him, "Friend, who set me to be a judge or arbitrator over you?" [15] And he said to them, "Take care! Be on your guard against all kinds of greed; for one's life does not consist in the abundance of possessions." [16] Then he told them a parable: "The land of a rich man produced abundantly. [17] And he thought to himself, 'What should I do, for I have no place to store my crops?' [18] Then he said, 'I will do this: I will pull down my barns and build larger ones, and there I will store all my grain and my goods. [19] And I will say to my soul, "Soul, you have ample goods laid up for many years; relax, eat, drink, be merry." ' [20] But God said to him, 'You fool! This very night your life is being demanded of you. And the things you have prepared, whose will they be?' [21] So it is with those who store up treasures for themselves but are not rich toward God."*

2. What's Happening?

First Point Of Action

Calling Jesus Teacher, someone in the crowd asks Jesus to tell his brother to divide the family inheritance with the man. Calling

95

the man Friend, Jesus wonders who set him to be a judge or arbitrator over him.

Second Point Of Action

Addressing the crowd, Jesus cautions them to be on their guard against all kinds of greed because our life does not consist in the abundance of possessions.

Third Point Of Action

Jesus tells the parable of The Rich Fool. A farmer has a great crop and not enough room to store it. He decides to tear down his barns and build bigger ones to store all of his grain and his goods. He then will tell his soul that since he has plenty stored up for many years, he can relax, eat, drink, and be merry.

Fourth Point Of Action

Continuing the parable, God tells him that he will die that very night. What good will his stored up goods do toward that?

Fifth Point Of Action

Jesus tells the crowd that is what happens to those who store up treasures for themselves but are not rich toward God.

3. Spadework

Arbitrate

To arbitrate, judge, determine, or decide the path for the greedy brother in the present parable was an intervention that Christ refused to make. His arbitration was for justice: "Speak out, judge righteously, defend the rights of the poor and needy" (Proverbs 31:9). "I will seek the lost, and I will bring back the strayed, and I will bind up the injured, and I will strengthen the weak, but the fat and the strong I will destroy. I will feed them with justice" (Ezekiel 34:16).

His arbitration was for peacemaking: "He shall judge between the nations, and shall arbitrate for many peoples; they shall beat their swords into plowshares, and their spears into pruning hooks;

96

nation shall not lift up sword against nation, neither shall they learn war any more" (Isaiah 2:4). See also Micah 4:3.

Through the voice of scripture, God offers guides for realigning our direction away from greed. One guideline is to get in touch with that integrity deep within us beneath the greed and the selfishness. "The Lord judges the peoples; judge me, O Lord, according to my righteousness and according to the integrity that is in me" (Psalm 7:8).

What would happen if we also were to follow these words? "... [D]o good, be rich in good works, generous, and ready to share, so [you] may take hold of the life that really is life" (1 Timothy 6:18, 19).

Personal fulfillment is available through other means than by squirreling away possessions: "Happy are those who observe justice, who do righteousness at all times" (Psalm 106:3). "It is well with those who deal generously and lend, who conduct their affairs with justice" (Psalm 112:5). "[L]earn to do good; seek justice, rescue the oppressed, defend the orphan, plead for the widow" (Isaiah 1:17).

"He has told you, O mortal, what is good; and what does the Lord require of you but to do justice, and to love kindness, and to walk humbly with your God?" (Micah 6:8).

Greed (greedy)

Greed is an insatiable craving that forgets about all else except acquiring more than one needs or deserves. Of the nine references to greed, Job 20:20-22 images the gluttony and the misery of greed: "They knew no quiet in their bellies; in their greed they let nothing escape. There was nothing left after they had eaten; therefore their prosperity will not endure. In full sufficiency they will be in distress; all the force of misery will come upon them." "[T]hey have grown fat and sleek. They know no limits in deeds of wickedness; they do not judge with justice the cause of the orphan, to make it prosper, and they do not defend the rights of the needy" (Jeremiah 5:28).

Matthew 23:25 and Luke 11:39 refer to the hypocrisy of the Pharisees who "clean the outside of the cup and of the plate, but inside [they][you] are full of greed and [self-indulgence][wickedness]."

In the New Testament letters, greed is improper among saints. Greed is earthly, idolatry, and leads to exploitation with deceptive words. The hearts of the ungodly are trained in greed. See Ephesians 5:3, Colossians 3:5, 1 Thessalonians 2:5, and 2 Peter 2:3 and 2:14.

"Greedy" occurs seventeen times. Psalm 10:3 and Proverbs 1:19 refer to being "greedy for gain." In 1 Samuel, the phrase is "look with greedy eye" (1 Samuel 2:29 and 2:32).

Throughout the Bible, an aborted life is the standard payment for a greedy nature. "Then in distress you will look with greedy eye on all the prosperity that shall be bestowed upon Israel; and no one in your family shall ever live to old age" (1 Samuel 2:32). "Such is the end of all who are greedy for gain; it takes away the life of its possessors" (Proverbs 1:19).

Those who are greedy "curse and renounce God" (Psalm 10:3). The greedy person "stirs up strife" (Proverbs 28:25).

Two couplets from Proverbs present a correction for greed: "Those who are greedy for unjust gain make trouble for their households, but those who hate bribes will live" (Proverbs 15:27) and "The greedy person stirs up strife, but whoever trusts in the Lord will be enriched" (Proverbs 28:25).

Is a modicum of greed universal to humanity? "For from the least to the greatest of them, everyone is greedy for unjust gain; and from prophet to priest, everyone deals falsely" (Jeremiah 6:13). See also Jeremiah 8:10.

The prophet Nehemiah suggests that eating is only part of celebrating. The other part of joy is sharing it: "Then he said to them, 'Go your way, eat the fat and drink sweet wine and send portions of them to those for whom nothing is prepared, for this day is holy to our Lord; and do not be grieved, for the joy of the Lord is your strength' " (Nehemiah 8:10).

What a thought Hosea stirs in suggesting that we are greedy for the dark side of ourselves: "They feed on the sin of my people; they are greedy for their iniquity" (Hosea 4:8). Greediness comes in a variety of forms: "greedy for money" (1 Timothy 3:8) or "greedy for gain" (Titus 1:7). See also 1 Corinthians 5:10-11 and 6:10 and Ephesians 4:19.

Greed can be defined as idolatry: "Be sure of this, that no fornicator or impure person, or one who is greedy (that is, an idolater), has any inheritance in the kingdom of Christ and of God" (Ephesians 5:5).

Idol

The second of the Ten Commandments reads, "You shall not make for yourself an idol, whether in the form of anything that is in heaven above, or that is on the earth beneath, or that is in the water under the earth" (Exodus 20:4).

Are the early, high-energy years the time we are particularly vulnerable to greed? We become the work-aholics, the play-aholics, and the cocoon-aholics. We make as much money as we can. We invest as much money as we can. We acquire as much stuff as we can. We give little thought to sharing our wealth, our goods, or our time with those who are impoverished. The more we get, the more we feel the weight of acquisition. What we do give to church, charity, or stranger is a laughable token.

Are the later years the time we are particularly vulnerable to greed? When we have "done our giving" in the raising of children and our children's children, paid off the mortgage and the college loans, and "become complacent in the land," we yield to doing for ourselves — a trophy house, an Alaskan cruise, eating an outrageous and unhealthy amount of food, still buying this and buying that to occupy the void within the heart, and generally acting "corruptly by making an idol in the form of anything, thus doing what is evil in the sight of the Lord your God ..." (from Deuteronomy 4:25).

Consider the "things" that accumulate for dusting in light of the words of the prophet Habakkuk: "What use is an idol once its maker has shaped it — a cast image, a teacher of lies? For its maker trusts in what has been made, though the product is only an idol that cannot speak!" (Habakkuk 2:18).

Consider the money wasted on an accumulation of memory treasures, collection after collection. The living memory of having shared that money in an act of kindness that improved the quality of another's life lies as an unexplored intangible treasure. "Put to death, therefore, whatever in you is earthly: fornication, impurity, passion, evil desire, and greed (which is idolatry)" (Colossians 3:5).

Is it possible to redirect our passions? If we contain a "greedy gene," is it possible to convert that energy into a life that really is life?

> *Thus says the Lord God: Ah, you shepherds of Israel who have been feeding yourselves! Should not shepherds feed the sheep? You eat the fat, you clothe yourselves with the wool, you slaughter the fatlings; but you do not feed the sheep. You have not strengthened the weak, you have not healed the sick, you have not bound up the injured, you have not brought back the strayed, you have not sought the lost, but with force and harshness you have ruled them.* — Ezekiel 34:2b-4

Possessions

There is a difference between a cache of hoarded possessions and the plentitude that is the reward of an observant God:

> *God answered Solomon, "Because this was in your heart, and you have not asked for possessions, wealth, honor, or the life of those who hate you, and have not even asked for long life, but have asked for wisdom and knowledge for yourself that you may rule my people over whom I have made you king, wisdom and knowledge are granted to you. I will also give you riches, possessions, and honor, such as none of the kings had who were before you, and none after you shall have the like."* — 2 Chronicles 1:11-12

Christ shows little understanding toward those who focus on material goods: Jesus said to the man who wanted to earn eternal life, " 'If you wish to be perfect, go, sell your possessions, and give the money to the poor, and you will have treasure in heaven; then come, follow me.' When the young man heard this word, he went away grieving, for he had many possessions" (Matthew 19:21-22); "Sell your possessions ..." (Luke 12:33a); "So therefore, none of

you can become my disciple if you do not give up all your possessions" (Luke 14:33).

While, according to the attitude above, Jesus would have pre-
ferred that Zacchaeus give up all his possessions, even a halfway
turn about was worthy of rejoicing: "Zacchaeus stood there and
said to the Lord, 'Look, half of my possessions, Lord, I will give to
the poor; and if I have defrauded anyone of anything, I will pay
back four times as much.' Then Jesus said to him, 'Today salvation
has come to this house, because he too is a son of Abraham. For the
Son of Man came to seek out and to save the lost' " (Luke19:8-10).

Paul reminds us that the life that is really life is about more
than even limiting one's material goods. The Pauline benchmark
reads, "If I give away all my possessions, and if I hand over my
body so that I may boast, but do not have love, I gain nothing" (1
Corinthians 13:3).

4. Parallel Scripture

On Taking Responsibility
Compare "But [Jesus] said to him, 'Friend, who set me to be a
judge or arbitrator over you?' " (Luke 12:14) with Jesus' words to
the crowd: "And why do you not judge for yourselves what is right?"
(Luke 12:57). (See Weather Signs, Parable 10, Cycle C.)

On The Life That Is Really Life
Compare "[F]or one's life does not consist in the abundance of
possessions" (Luke 12:16) with "[D]o good, be rich in good works,
generous, and ready to share, so [you] may take hold of the life
that really is life" (1 Timothy 6:18-19); "If I give away all my possessions, and if I hand over my body so that I may boast, but do not
have love, I gain nothing" (1 Corinthians 13:3).

The Futility Of Greed
Compare "But God said to him, 'You fool! This very night your
life is being demanded of you. And the things you have prepared,
whose will they be?' So it is with those who store up treasures for

themselves but are not rich toward God" (Luke 12:20-21) with the following:

"Now the end is upon you ... I will judge you according to your ways" (Ezekiel 7:3);

"They knew no quiet in their bellies; in their greed they let nothing escape. There was nothing left after they had eaten; therefore their prosperity will not endure. In full sufficiency they will be in distress; all the force of misery will come upon them" (Job 20:20-22);

"Then in distress you will look with greedy eye on all the prosperity that shall be bestowed upon Israel; and no one in your family shall ever live to old age" (1 Samuel 2:32); and

"Be sure of this, that no fornicator or impure person, or one who is greedy (that is, an idolater), has any inheritance in the kingdom of Christ and of God" (Ephesians 5:5).

5. Chat Room

Doug: Hey, Sandy, are you logged on? Hey, anyway, is double heart disease one of the rewards of a subtle greed?

Sandy: Double heart disease? I get it about the physical heart disease from the glut of food and the pressure of the quest. What is this "double" about?

Doug: The sickness in my soul that keeps me pushing any way and every way for more while becoming less satisfied and less satisfied and less satisfied, that is

> Greedy for inner peace,
> Greedy for prestige,
> Greedy for retirement,
> Greedy for praise,
> Greedy for comfort.
>
> Power-hungry,
> Space-hungry,

Activity-hungry,
Friend-starved.

Empty-hearted.
Soul-less.

Sandy: I see, not that other greed of

Eat, drink, be merry,
Material things,
Treasures, riches,
Stuff, stuff, and more stuff,
Clout,
Preparing forever,
Worrying without end.

How many vehicles is enough
How many acres
Houses
How much preparation
How much fun
How many invested dollars?

When is enough, enough?

Bryce: Okay, you two poets. Enough is enough. Sounds as if you have a good case of a tipped Protestant work ethic.

Sandy: Tipped Protestant work ethic?

Bryce: You know, the moral value of work, thrift, and our individual responsibility for our actions. I started out okay, myself. From youth, I knew how to work hard. I took my training and began my career. I took responsibility. I thrived.

You remember your first paycheck, don't you? It was mine, all mine. I earned it. I couldn't wait to buy something with it. I was hooked. I became more responsible. I began to save a portion, then saved more and more, but there was so much I wanted to buy. Then it all mushroomed. I had to work more and more to afford what I wanted. I know when enthusiasm turned into passion. I'm still not sure when passion crossed the line to become greed.

It looked good on the outside. On the inside, every other dimension of my life was suffering — my body, family, relationships, my soul. It was not what I had hoped for. It was advancing me all right — parading me right toward death.

Doug: So how did you get things back into balance?

Bryce: I had caught on to the work part of the work ethic but missed the thrift aspect. It had seemed unnecessary. What was unnecessary was the way I spent money, time, energy, and, most of all, my gifts and human resources. I began to examine my idols, the little gods in my life that had grown great with false stature. I started to ask questions before I did anything — Why? Are you sure? For what purpose, really? What is the benefit? I asked these questions about what I ate, how I played, how I related to others, how I spent myself.

Doug: What about hope? Why can't someone intervene in our lives before we become hopeless, before it is too late? We botch things awfully because we are free spirits. Then we pay the consequences of a spiritually corrupt day-to-day living style.

Sandy: That's the point. That's where the responsibility dimension of the work ethic comes in. I'm a free spirit, free to make the right choices, free to make the wrong decisions, free to harvest the result, but I am created free. That's what makes the times of turnaround fascinating. We are little different from Zacchaeus.

You asked what moves us to hope. I find hope is within the surprise, in the supposed incongruity and the paradox. Where is the surprise? Less is more. Simpler is richer. Giving is receiving. Downsizing in every area. Raising a few notches higher the level of a simpler lifestyle. Giving more than hoarding. Taking the sharing alternative to storing.

The dimension of my soul that needed tending found healing by giving myself. I switched some of that run-ragged time to volunteering in a one-to-one project. I discovered that I was still alive in there. I discovered the fun of helping to awaken joy in others and watching them also come to a more meaningful life. My own double heart disease began to heal itself. It has become the best time of my life.

Parable 9

Watching Servants

Luke 12:32-40

---

1. Text

"Do not be afraid, little flock, for it is your Father's good pleasure to give you the kingdom. [33] Sell your possessions, and give alms. Make purses for yourselves that do not wear out, an unfailing treasure in heaven, where no thief comes near and no moth destroys. [34] For where your treasure is, there your heart will be also.

[35] "Be dressed for action and have your lamps lit; [36] be like those who are waiting for their master to return from the wedding banquet, so that they may open the door for him as soon as he comes and knocks. [37] Blessed are those slaves whom the master finds alert when he comes; truly I tell you, he will fasten his belt and have them sit down to eat, and he will come and serve them. [38] If he comes during the middle of the night, or near dawn, and finds them so, blessed are those slaves.

[39] "But know this: if the owner of the house had known at what hour the thief was coming, he would not have let his house be broken into. [40] You also must be ready, for the Son of Man is coming at an unexpected hour."

2. What's Happening?

First Point Of Action

Jesus reassures.

Second Point Of Action
Jesus speaks about possessions and treasure.

Third Point Of Action
He advises his listeners to maintain a state of alertness at all times, like watchful servants waiting for the return of their master.

Fourth Point Of Action
The master rewards the faithful servant.

Fifth Point Of Action
One cannot know when the thief will break into the house. Jesus interprets that the coming of the Son of Man is also at an unexpected hour.

3. Spadework

Action
Since 9/11, we have moved closer to grasping the feeling tone of the early Christians who did not know precisely what to expect but anticipated something of catastrophic dimension. The necessary action of readiness is twofold. First, be dressed for action. Be ready. Then give a sign that you are ready. Put a light in your window. Should you live in earthquake land, keep hearing aids or glasses in a secured container beside your bed. Second, communicate what others need to know to those persons who are important to you. Show a trusted person in another apartment the location of your diabetic supplies. Plan signals and alternative escape routes with neighbors. The preparedness list is extensive.

Being "dressed for action" involves more than keeping a pair of shoes and a set of sweats beside the bed during tornado season. Dressed for action implies having made the choice to meet whatever comes with the vigor and attitude of one who is fully present in spirit. The light in the window tells others of your presence as it invites and welcomes. Being prepared and letting others know it involves a partnership of caring, both giving and receiving.

Do Not Be Afraid

If not with fear, then how should one greet the unexpected coming of the Son of Man? Christ's choice of imagery carries a note of tension that interlaces with enthusiastic anticipation. Being apprehensive suggests being filled with fear or concern. It also may indicate being unwilling to do something. Disquietude opposes a sense of peace.

This parable characterizes the pull between the fear of the unknown and its concurrent sense of inadequacy for meeting that unknown and the determination to choose hope over fear. The latter choice requires trust and the faithfulness to stay the course of inner strength that will result in a sense of peace. Such a choice of attitude fortifies one for the unknown without being foolhardy. Among the eighty biblical references from Genesis to Revelation to not being afraid are Psalm 85:13, Psalm 89:14, Isaiah 41:10, Isaiah 45:2, Isaiah 52:12, Isaiah 58:8, Jeremiah 1:8, and Mark 14:28.

Christ has a way of calling us to responsibility while also speaking to our innermost uncertainties. This marriage of challenge, which nudges us forward, and of reassurance, which energizes our tenacity, enables us to remember that God goes before us always. "And remember, I am with you always, to the end of the age" (Matthew 28:20b).

Give Alms

One immediate surprise of this parable is Christ's instruction to the disciples not only to sell their possessions but also to give alms. One would have surmised that by selling one's possessions, nothing would remain for giving alms. The seller would need the profit to exist. Earlier in Luke however, speaking to the Pharisees who practiced everything to the letter but missed the action of the heart, Christ instructed, "So give for alms those things that are within" (Luke 11:41a). There are other ways to give voluntarily to the poor than giving money; giving of one's time and acts of service, to name two.

Further, Matthew clarifies the appropriate way to give alms, that is, in a quiet manner unlike the praise-seeking "hypocrites in the synagogues and in the streets" who draw attention to themselves. Matthew adds, "But when you give alms, do not let your left hand know what your right hand is doing, so that your alms may be done in secret; and your Father who sees in secret will reward you" (Matthew 6:2-4).

Little Flock

The message of the gentle caring of these words addressed first to those whom Jesus loved somehow also enfolds present-day hearers. Something within us also needs comforting even in the midst of activity and fullness of life. We also need the reminder that we are part of a treasured flock guided by a shepherd.

The New Testament image of flock begins with Luke's initial voice of the angel telling the shepherds who were "keeping watch over their flock by night" (Luke 2:8). In today's parable is Luke's recording of Jesus' words of reassurance and his reminder that God means well for followers.

Through the pastoral metaphor, the author of the Gospel of John offers the vision of a sense of community: "I have other sheep that do not belong to this fold. I must bring them also, and they will listen to my voice. So there will be one flock, one shepherd" (John 10:16).

Building upon the words of the prophet Jeremiah, "Jesus said to them, 'You will all become deserters because of me this night; for it is written, "I will strike the shepherd, and the sheep of the flock will be scattered" ' " (Matthew 26:31). The Jeremiah text reads:

> *Therefore thus saith the Lord God of Israel against the pastors that feed my people; Ye have scattered my flock, and driven them away, and have not visited them: behold, I will visit upon you the evil of your doings, saith the Lord. And I will gather the remnant of my flock out of all countries whither I have driven them, and will bring them again to their folds; and they shall be fruitful and increase.* — Jeremiah 23:2-3 (KJV)
> (See also Jeremiah 10:21.)

110

Of the 95 biblical references to "flock," Job, the Psalmist, and the Prophets use the term as a metaphor. Jeremiah uses the metaphor eight times. See Jeremiah 13:17, 13:20, 25:34-36, 31:10-12, 49:20, 50:8, and 50:45. As early as Genesis, "shepherd" appears as a metaphor: "He blessed Joseph, and said, 'The God before whom my ancestors Abraham and Isaac walked, the God who has been my shepherd all my life to this day' " (Genesis 48:15). However, in the canonical sequence of the Old Testament, Job is the first to use "flock" as a metaphor. (See Job 21:11.)

While only Psalms 68:10, 77:20, 78:52, and 79:13—80:1 use the direct word, "flock," the Twenty-third Psalm sings with singular emphasis. "Shepherd" occurs 53 other times in the Bible. The Prophets refer to "flock" on 33 occasions, led by Isaiah who begins with the familiar "Messiah" text: "He will feed his flock like a shepherd; he will gather the lambs in his arms, and carry them in his bosom, and gently lead the mother sheep" (Isaiah 40:11). But who not living in rural areas thinks about sheep today?

Serve The Slaves

Jesus is an artist at the tool of surprise. When the master returns home, he will have the servants sit down and the master will serve them with gratitude for their readiness. The message: There is recompense for having done the work of our life well, although it may come in an unanticipated form.

Unexpected

The bond of the unexpected, the states of anxiety and of uncertainty, and the constant tension of not knowing when the anticipated will happen can play havoc with one's entire being. Herbert Benson, author of *The Relaxation Response*,[1] awakens us to awareness of the unhealthy physical and psychological consequences of living in a constant, ready-to-spring attitude. Consider the alternative of preparing for the unexpected so we can be ready. Able to relax, we can save the adrenalin for the appropriate time rather than constantly drawing it through our entire system and depleting physical, spiritual, and emotional resources.

3. Parallel Scripture

State Of Alertness

Luke says, "Be dressed for action and have your lamps lit" (Luke 12:35) and "You also must be ready" (Luke 12:40). For another reference to the state of alert readiness for the coming of God's realm, see Cycle C, Parable 1, The Sign Of The Fig Tree. The writer of Mark uses the term, "keep awake" (Mark 13:35). Earlier, Mark says, "Beware, keep alert; for you do not know when the time will come" (Mark 13:33). In the parable of the bridesmaids and the lamps, Jesus says, "Keep awake therefore, for you know neither the day nor the hour" (Matthew 25:13). (See Cycle A, Parable 12, The Wise And The Foolish, Matthew 25:1ff.) Warning that the kingdom of God was near, Jesus says, "Be on guard ..." (Luke 21:34).

Do Not Be Afraid

This phrase of reassurance appears 66 times in the Bible. Of the sixteen Gospel references, five were spoken by an angel messenger bringing unsettling news. These were the first words the angel said to Joseph then to Mary, to Zechariah, to the shepherds on the hillside, and to the women at the Tomb. (See Matthew 1:20, 28:5; Luke 1:13, 1:30, and 2:10.) First, begin by quieting your fears. Then, hear what I have to say. The recorded sources tell us that Jesus spoke these words eleven times. (See Matthew 10:31, 14:27, 17:7, 28:5, 28:10; Mark 6:50; Luke 5:10, 12:7, 12:32; and John 6:20 and 12:15.)

Within the context of the death of the Centurion's daughter, Jesus calmed, "Do not fear, only believe" (Mark 5:36). Again through the later interpretation of the Gospel according to John, Jesus counters fear with a sense of peace: "Peace I leave with you; my peace I give to you. I do not give to you as the world gives. Do not let your hearts be troubled, and do not let them be afraid" (John 14:27), and "I have said this to you, so that in me you may have peace. In the world you face persecution. But take courage; I have conquered the world!" (John 16:33).

The Faithful Servant

"Blessed are those slaves whom the master finds alert when he comes; truly I tell you, he will fasten his belt and have them sit down to eat, and he will come and serve them" (Luke 12:37). In Matthew, the pleased master will "put that [faithful slave] in charge of all his possessions" (Matthew 24:27), while he will come to the wicked slave at an unexpected hour and "cut him in pieces and put him with the hypocrites, where there will be weeping and gnashing of teeth" (Matthew 24:26).

Time Of The Coming

Luke says the coming will be at an "unexpected hour" (Luke 12:40). In Cycle C, Parable 1, Luke suggests the coming is not entirely unexpected. Alert people will notice and pay attention to signs of change. However, they must remain attentive lest "that day catch [them] unexpectedly" (Luke 21:34). Luke refers in this parable to "the middle of the night, or near dawn" (Luke 21:38), while Mark says, "[Y]ou do not know when the master of the house will come, in the evening, or at midnight, or at cockcrow, or at dawn" (Mark 13:35).

Treasure

Both Luke and Matthew use "For where your treasure is, there your heart will be also." (See Luke 12:34 and Matthew 6:21.) Luke says, "where ... no moth destroys (Luke 12:33). Matthew says, "where moth and rust consume" (Matthew 6:19). Luke couches the metaphor in the positive, "Make purses for yourselves ..." (Luke 12:34), whereas Matthew's initial statement is the negative, "Do not store up for yourselves" (Matthew 6:19). Matthew completes the thought in the positive mode. Luke says, "where no thief comes near" (Luke 12:33), and Matthew says, "where thieves break in and steal" (Matthew 6:19). See also the "Consider the lilies" passage about not worrying in Matthew 6:25-33.

5. Chat Room

Brent: Isn't all of this talk about edge of the chair expectation of the coming realm of God outmoded? Wasn't this a ploy to keep people interested in a time they easily could have become passive and simply let go of this new way of living, the Christian way? Contemplating the ending of the world is exciting stuff. While some among us still are caught in predicting the time line of a sudden, world-ending saga, has that not become passe? Having said that, I shudder again at recent memory of human-made disasters that have made such possibilities unexpectedly personal.

Tom: A greater truth gives this parable its continued validity. This parable tells us a lot about God. It tells us about ourselves, about being responsible. The pull still exists between the giving of God's realm on earth and our readiness to receive it. No matter what, God always responds first to the person with these words, "Do not be afraid."

Brent: That is revealing about God. It tells us that God's first concern is to connect at the level of heart. We have so many things to be afraid of today. All sorts of anxiety ramp from the east to the west coast of the North American continent, from ocean to ocean to ocean around the world. Imaginations flare with possible threats. Fear makes complacency shiver.

D.P.: May I join this chat? I am a member of a disaster preparedness committee in our church. I make an analogy between this parable and the possibility of a present day disaster. Disaster preparedness is among the hardest things for most persons to manage. Something inside us resists. We put off becoming as prepared as possible even though we know we are not exempt from an emergency that could make complete chaos out of life as usual.

Brent: Our human nature does tend to ascribe to the head-in-the-sand philosophy, whether it is about preparing for the unforeseen disaster or living as we ought.

D.P.: The moment the evacuation of a town is announced because of a toxic spill caused by the derailment of the 9:20 freight is no time to begin the search for something to put the cat in, get an extra supply of my medications from the pharmacist, and arrange for alternative transportation because my vehicle is in the shop.

Brent: After your son has impregnated his girl friend is no time to talk to him about respecting the being of a woman. After your wife has filed for divorce is a little late to decide to pay more attention to the relationship. When you are having your heart attack —

Tom: I get the idea.

D.P.: Our church folk have disaster readiness partnerships with members who are vulnerable. Beyond preparing, we need to communicate our needs to those who can help or who are important to us as well as letting them know how we have prepared. Becoming as prepared as possible keeps fear in its place. It keeps our lives in perspective. Following guidelines for preparedness keeps a positive focus.

Tom: That also would follow for adhering to the requirements for living within God's realm on earth.

Brent: Are you assuming that the coming of the realm of God is negative and destructive? Consider the effect of what one anticipates with such a coming. If I perceive it primarily from the stance of one who is guilty of numerous shortfalls, then I might see it as a negative coming.

Tom: I may be misinterpreting or even rationalizing, however, I see the realm of God as a nudge, a spiritual realization where people increasingly respect each other. Whenever and wherever we see the promotion of basic human rights, when we increase international cooperation and understanding, and when we move beyond selfishness and self-interest, we further the presence of the realm of God.

D.P.: There will always be the negative comings: tornados, floods, anthrax, the next pipe bomb in the mailbox down the road, whatever it is that is coming next. We can become depleted by fear, or we can take an attitude that counteracts the paralysis of fright.

Brent: If we could return to the parable, another aspect enters here. What do you have to say about not only the slave's invitation to sit down at the owner's table but the owner's serving the servant? It is like a warrior from the opposing side taking time out from the war to locate a new pair of shoes for an "enemy" warrior. It is like a foreman on the assembly line volunteering to fill in for a faithful line worker the last two hours of the shift.

Tom: I think there also is another point. God appreciates our faithfulness. God recognizes our having enough concern for another person to ignore the differences between the two of you, to connect soul to soul. God rewards such devotion to what is right. In the service sector of society, the kind of personal care that grows from human concern and respect puts the person first. It is good business. Furthermore, it is good for the soul. It affirms the intrinsic value of the whole human family.

Brent: So what does this parable tell us about how we are to prepare our inner lives for the coming of the realm of God?

Tom: Well, I'd say do your best to be responsible about following the Two Commandments. It is relationship, relationship, relationship with God, with others, and with ourselves. God will notice. Let the rest take care of itself.

Brent: So the moral of the story is to be alert always to how you are living. Keep eye, ear, and heart open. Pay attention to how you go about your business. God will reward your faithfulness beyond what you would expect and probably when you least expect. If we live in this way, we may discover that what we treasure has little to do with money or worldly goods. Its center lies with the intangible qualities of the heart that can exist regardless of the externals.

Tom: God is as generous as the generous owner of the servant. It always has a reciprocal element, doesn't it? The ancient rainbow covenant between God and us always is two-way.

Brent: If we come through, God will come through. Perhaps we can come through *because* we can trust that God will come through. I don't think this parable is about fear after all. "It is your Father's good pleasure to give you the kingdom," Jesus said. But look out if you are irresponsible.

---

1. Herbert Benson, *The Relaxation Response*, (New York: Morrow, William and Company, 2000).

Parable 10

Weather Signs

Luke 12:49-56

---

1. Text

> *"I came to bring fire to the earth, and how I wish it were already kindled! [50] I have a baptism with which to be baptized, and what stress I am under until it is completed! [51] Do you think that I have come to bring peace to the earth? No, I tell you, but rather division! [52] From now on five in one household will be divided, three against two and two against three; [53] they will be divided: father against son and son against father, mother against daughter and daughter against mother, mother-in-law against her daughter-in-law and daughter-in-law against mother-in-law."*
>
> *[54] He also said to the crowds, "When you see a cloud rising in the west, you immediately say, 'It is going to rain'; and so it happens. [55] And when you see the south wind blowing, you say, 'There will be scorching heat'; and it happens. [56] You hypocrites! You know how to interpret the appearance of earth and sky, but why do you not know how to interpret the present time?"*

2. What's Happening?

First Point Of Action

During his talking to the crowds, Jesus addresses the disciples as an aside. He says his purpose is to bring fire to the earth. He wishes it were already kindled.

119

Second Point Of Action

Jesus says he has a baptism with which to be baptized. Again, he says how stressed he will be until it is completed.

Third Point Of Action

Jesus asks if they think he has come to bring peace to the earth. He says an emphatic no. He has come to bring division.

Fourth Point Of Action

Jesus describes the division as within households, citing a family of five will be divided three against two and two against three. He then lists reciprocal, familial relationships — father/son, mother/daughter, mother-in-law/daughter-in-law.

Fifth Point Of Action

Jesus tells the crowds the Parable of the Weather Signs. If they see clouds rising in the west, they correctly predict rain. If they observe a south wind, they correctly predict that the weather will be scorching.

Sixth Point Of Action

Jesus calls them hypocrites.

Seventh Point Of Action

He asks if they can interpret future events of the earth and sky, why then can they not interpret what they see is happening around them in the present time?

3. Spadework

Baptize (Baptism)

With nineteen references, baptism is a term exclusive to the New Testament. When the scribes and Pharisees questioned Christ's authority, they asked about the source of the baptism of John. "Did the baptism of John come from heaven, or was it of human origin?" Understanding their trick, Jesus refused to answer. See Matthew 21:25 and Mark 11:30.

All five Gospel references to "baptize" refer to the baptism John offered. "Did the baptism of John come from heaven, or was it of human origin?" (Luke 20:4). John carefully differentiates between his baptism and Christ's. "I have baptized you with water; but he will baptize you with the Holy Spirit" (Mark 1:8).

"And when Jesus had been baptized [by John], just as he came up from the water, suddenly the heavens were opened to him and he saw the Spirit of God descending like a dove and alighting on him. And a voice from heaven said, 'This is my Son, the Beloved, with whom I am well pleased' " (see Matthew 3:13-17).

When the people wondered if John were the Messiah, "John answered all of them by saying, 'I baptize you with water; but one who is more powerful than I is coming; I am not worthy to untie the thong of his sandals. He will baptize you with the Holy Spirit and fire' " (Luke 3:16 and Matthew 3:11). "I myself did not know him, but the one who sent me to baptize with water said to me, 'He on whom you see the Spirit descend and remain is the one who baptizes with the Holy Spirit' " (John 1:33). John's baptism with water was a baptism of repentance for the forgiveness of sins. (See Matthew 3:7; Mark 1:4; Luke 3:3, 7:29, and 20:4; and Acts 1:22, 10:37, 13:24, and 19:3-4.)

Today's parable and the following text are the only two references Jesus makes to "baptism" or "baptized." When James and John asked to sit "in glory" to the right and left of Jesus, "Jesus said to them, 'You do not know what you are asking. Are you able to drink the cup that I drink, or be baptized with the baptism that I am baptized with?' They replied, 'We are able.' " Jesus told them that was not for him to decide. "Then Jesus said to them, 'The cup that I drink you will drink; and with the baptism with which I am baptized, you will be baptized' " (Mark 10:38-39).

The author of Acts describes the "burning enthusiasm" of Apollos, suggesting Christ's baptism is related to the Pentecost spirit: "[Apollos] had been instructed in the Way of the Lord; and he spoke with *burning enthusiasm* and taught accurately the things concerning Jesus, though he knew only the baptism of John" (Acts 18:25).

Division

We expect Jesus to bring reconciliation, peace, and cooperation. He surprises by announcing that he brings division. Furthermore, that division, at least in households, is to be "from now on." (See Luke 12:52.) Not only will there be division, according to Matthew "one's foes will be members of one's own household" (Matthew 10:36).

Does the chaos of division and its accompanying falling apart of relationships and getting rid of what no longer is of value always have to precede the growth and progress that positive change brings? Does disintegration always have to preface integration whether within a society, a family, or an individual?

Do the next three verses of this Matthean passage bring more understanding of this division? "Whoever loves father or mother more than me is not worthy of me; and whoever loves son or daughter more than me is not worthy of me; and whoever does not take up the cross and follow me is not worthy of me. Those who find their life will lose it, and those who lose their life for my sake will find it" (Matthew 10:37-39). Because various members of a household will want to follow Christ, they will need to make difficult, family-disrupting choices.

Fire

In today's text, Jesus said he came to bring fire to the earth. Does Jesus mean the fire that purifies? Does he mean the fire that brings the power of the Holy Spirit? His telling the disciples, "[H]ow I wish that it were already kindled" (Luke 12:49), suggests a destructive yet cleansing preparatory fire.

Most of the 406 biblical references to fire occur in the early Hebrew law books and refer to the prescribed fire of burning food sacrifices and those in the place of worship. For example, "You shall kindle no fire in all your dwellings on the sabbath day" (Exodus 35:3) and "A perpetual fire shall be kept burning on the altar; it shall not go out" (Leviticus 6:13).

Fire was associated in both constructive and destructive ways with God. God used "a pillar of fire by night" to give the wandering Hebrews light. (See Exodus 13:21-22.) When God appeared at

Mount Sinai, God "had descended upon it in fire; the smoke went up like the smoke of a kiln, while the whole mountain shook violently" (Exodus 19:18). "Fire came out from the Lord and consumed the burnt offering and the fat on the altar; and when all the people saw it, they shouted and fell on their faces" (Leviticus 9:24).

God's voice comes as fire. "Then the Lord spoke to you out of the fire. You heard the sound of words but saw no form; there was only a voice" (Deuteronomy 4:12). See also Deuteronomy 4:36 and Psalm 29:7. God, however, did not come as fire to Elijah: "... and after the earthquake a fire, but the Lord was not in the fire; and after the fire a sound of sheer silence" (1 Kings 19:12).

Fire was used for purification. "[E]verything that can withstand fire, shall be passed through fire, and it shall be clean. Nevertheless it shall also be purified with the water for purification; and whatever cannot withstand fire, shall be passed through the water" (Numbers 31:23).

When the Hebrews were cautioned to avoid provoking God to anger by forgetting the covenant and making idols to worship, God was described as "a devouring fire, a jealous God" (Deuteronomy 4:23-26). See also Psalm 50:3. "For a fire is kindled by my anger, and burns to the depths of Sheol; it devours the earth and its increase, and sets on fire the foundations of the mountains" (Deuteronomy 32:22).

The prophets also use the imagery of God and fire. "[Y]ou will be visited by the Lord of hosts with thunder and earthquake and great noise, with whirlwind and tempest, and the flame of a devouring fire" (Isaiah 29:6) and "Is not my word like fire, says the Lord, and like a hammer that breaks a rock in pieces?" (Jeremiah 23:29).

In the New Testament, John speaks of Christ's baptizing of us "with the Holy Spirit and fire" (Matthew 3:11 and Luke 3:16). Metaphorically as well as literally, Jesus said, "Every tree that does not bear good fruit is cut down and thrown into the fire" (Matthew 7:19). Jesus will not allow his disciples James and John to invoke the power of fire to save him from the Jerusalem journey. (See Luke 9:54-55.) In the Pentecost story, fire represents the Holy Spirit: "Divided tongues, as of fire, appeared among them, and a tongue rested on each of them" (Acts 2:3).

Household

Of the 81 biblical references to "household," God's instruction to Noah is the first usage of the term: "Then the Lord said to Noah, 'Go into the ark, you and all your household, for I have seen that you alone are righteous before me in this generation' " (Genesis 7:1). More than the immediate family, a household included support people as well as servants. A large household, subject to the decisions of its head, was enviable. (See also Genesis 26:14 and 36:6, Joshua 24:15, and John 8:35.)

Hypocrite (Hypocrisy)

Matthew speaks of hypocrisy: "So you also on the outside look righteous to others, but inside you are full of hypocrisy and lawlessness" (Matthew 23:28). Hypocrites hold to beliefs, virtues, or feelings that we do not practice. Falseness, phoniness, pretense, and play-acting are all part of hypocrisy. Biblically, "hypocrite(s)" occurs eighteen times. Aside from Psalm 26, that addresses walking with integrity, these are found in the Synoptic Gospels. See, "I do not consort with the worthless, / nor do I consort with hypocrites" (Psalm 26:4).

Matthew 6:2, 6:5, and 6:16 refer obliquely to the Pharisees. Answering their challenges, Jesus calls the Pharisees and scribes hypocrites in Matthew 7:5, 15:7, and 22:18 and Luke 13:15. In Matthew 23:13, 23, 25, 27, and 29, he uses the "woe to you scribes and Pharisees, hypocrites" phrase. The writer of Matthew suggests what will happen to hypocrites. "He will cut him in pieces and put him with the hypocrites, where there will be weeping and gnashing of teeth" (Matthew 24:51).

In Luke 12:56, today's parable, Jesus may have used "hypocrite" for the benefit of church leaders who were among the crowd. Luke also records Jesus as having said, "Or how can you say to your neighbor, 'Friend, let me take out the speck in your eye,' when you yourself do not see the log in your own eye? You hypocrite, first take the log out of your own eye, and then you will see clearly to take the speck out of your neighbor's eye" (Luke 6:42). In these two passages, reader identification with hypocrisy is easier.

Mark quotes Jesus as answering the scribes and Pharisees, "Isaiah prophesied rightly about you hypocrites, as it is written, 'This people honors me with their lips but their hearts are far from me' " (Mark 7:6). The entire passage from Isaiah offers a fuller understanding of hypocrisy:

> *The Lord said: Because these people draw near with their mouths and honor me with their lips, while their hearts are far from me, and their worship of me is a human commandment learned by rote; so I will again do amazing things with this people, shocking and amazing. The wisdom of their wise shall perish, and the discernment of the discerning shall be hidden.*
>
> *Ha! You who hide a plan too deep for the Lord, whose deeds are in the dark, and who say, "Who sees us? Who knows us?" You turn things upside down!*
>
> — Isaiah 29:13-16a

Interpret

Of eleven references to "interpret," Genesis 40:8, 41:8, and 41:15 and Daniel 5:12 speak of dream interpretation. The writer of Daniel suggests that "an excellent spirit, knowledge, and understanding to interpret dreams, explain riddles, and solve problems" are requisite to any form of interpretation. (See Daniel 5:12.)

Regarding interpretation of the Law, the Deuteronomist advises: "You must carry out fully the law that [the levitical priests] interpret for you or the ruling that they announce to you; do not turn aside from the decision that they announce to you, either to the right or to the left" (Deuteronomy 17:11).

Using "interpret" in words recorded by Matthew and Luke, Jesus speaks of interpreting weather signs and what is happening in the human atmosphere of real life. (See Matthew 16:3.)

Most of the 27 references to "interpretation," including the sixteen found in Daniel, refer to dream interpretation. However the philosopher asks the leading question, "Who is like the wise man? And who knows the interpretation of a thing?" (Ecclesiastes 8:1a).

Relationships

Are the three troublesome, reciprocal relationships that Jesus cites of father/son, mother/daughter, and mother-in-law/daughter-in-law not the universal trouble spots for those vying for position? Jealousy, competition, and expectations keep the players in these relationships in a state of emotional disarray. We expect Jesus to be talking about the world situation or at least the political/historical circumstances or possibly the state of the human soul. Instead, he surprises us by describing the coming turmoil in terms of division within familial relationships. What does this say about where trouble begins, where we can make a difference, and where we must begin in order to improve relationships among the entire human family?

Has not, rather, the question of the human family been, "How long?"

> *How Long?*[1]
>
> *How long must we wait, God,*
> *for people to stop fighting*
> *nations and nations*
> *buyers and sellers*
> *the big ones and the little ones*
> *in-laws and relatives*
> *husbands and wives*
> *sisters and brothers*
> *for me to stop fighting with me?*
>
> *How long must we wait, God,*
> *before we let the Christ Child*
> *come here?*

4. Parallel Scripture

Baptize (Baptism)

"I have a baptism with which to be baptized" (Luke 12:50). John said, "He will baptize you with the Holy Spirit and fire" (Matthew 3:11c).

Interpret

Luke 12:56 reads, "You hypocrites! You know how to interpret the appearance of earth and sky, but why do you not know how to interpret the present time?" Matthew phrases this as a statement rather than as a query: "And in the morning, 'It will be stormy today, for the sky is red and threatening.' You know how to interpret the appearance of the sky, but you cannot interpret the signs of the times" (Matthew 16:3).

Relationships

In Luke, three troublesome, reciprocal relationships are listed as father/son, mother/daughter, and mother-in-law/daughter-in-law. (See Luke 12:53.) Matthew lists only the younger to older relationship direction of these three. Matthew adds, "and one's foes will be members of one's own household" (Matthew 10:36).

Division

Both Luke and Matthew speak of division within the household. Luke lists the division first in terms of a household of five: "From now on five in one household will be divided, three against two and two against three; they will be divided ..." (Luke 12:52-53). Matthew prefaces his list with "For I have come to set ..." (Matthew 10:35).

Statement Of Goal

In Luke, Christ states his purpose as a question that he answers: "Do you think that I have come to bring peace to the earth? No, I tell you, but rather division!" (Luke 12:51). In Matthew, Christ begins the segment by making a double declarative statement: "Do not think that I have come to bring peace to the earth; I have not come to bring peace, but a sword" (Matthew 10:34).

Peace

In the Matthean passage, Jesus uses "peace" twice then adds "sword": "Do not think that I have come to bring peace to the earth; I have not come to bring peace, but a sword" (Matthew 10:35).

5. Chat Room

John: For me, this parable raises more questions than it resolves. I am uncomfortable with the image of Jesus I find in the parable. He sounds stressed out. He sounds angry. He sounds like he uses the word "hypocrite" as a catch-all term when he is unhappy with something. He is wound up here, and he is just beginning his tirade. Why would Jesus say these things? To me, it sounds like a time of sheer chaos.

Alicia: It is. Jesus poses not one but two intriguing questions: "Do you think that I have come to bring peace?" he asks. Well, I thought so. And then he asks if we can figure out so easily the signs of weather change, why can we not interpret present time? Well, do we ever want to see the consequences of our actions while we can still remedy them?

Everyone, everywhere, would rather no one disturbed the water. That is how we are made. Prophets in all times call people to take responsibility for our actions. They do not want us to be passive. Prophets are hard to listen to. Jesus is the prophetic shepherd here who prods and jars us. We would much rather he were the great encourager.

Haley: Have you never been under a stress almost too great to carry? Jesus was feeling human feelings here. He was aware also of his divine calling. When do these natures conflict within you? (Yes, I believe we all have a divine purpose.) Who are the people with whom you are quite free to speak and with whom you are more guarded?

Alicia: If you are naturally a peacemaker, as I believe Jesus was, the task of stirring people into awareness is of particular difficulty. Real peace requires untying each knot of discord, one by one. That process can uncover more discord. Peacemaking is complex. Jesus' honesty to his disciples tells me a lot about myself.

If I can speak aloud to a trusted person the truth of how things are with me, I get that awful tension out of my system. Then I can set about the task of doing whatever it is that I do not want to do but know I must accomplish.

John: I fail to see why Jesus uses the word "hypocrite" here. Does he address the Pharisees in the crowds at this point? Just because we easily predict the weather from weather signs does not mean that we can as easily make the right call by the way people are acting. To be honest, I feel as if he were addressing me and all of my shortcomings. I fall short of my ideals.

Haley: I am neither mystery writer nor mystery solver. I simply do not notice things that seem obvious once they are pointed out to me. On the one hand, that allows me to concentrate on what is of most importance in my life. On the other hand, it keeps me from focusing on things that should carry more importance.

John: I still am uncertain what Jesus is trying to tell us here. He seems to be warning us. Is he telling us to stop short and take stock of how we live? Is he telling us that we must become more responsible for how we live? Does he foretell something awful that will happen in our world that we can no longer prevent because we have already messed up too much? Is he telling us that something really good will happen to us with the baptism of the Holy Spirit but that life will become bizarre first?

Haley: Do you ever stop asking questions?

John: Sorry, I'm just thinking aloud.

Alicia: Knowledgeable people have told us for some time that we need to take care of the earth or meet harmful consequences. We need to pay attention to the health of our relationships before they deteriorate too far to be saved. We need to take care of our body before a course of trouble becomes set. We need to do the nitty gritty of taking care of our children before addressing their problems becomes futile.

John: Why does Jesus use the familial relationships to speak of the discord that will happen? I keep thinking about the suffering of families in Jerusalem, Bethlehem, and all those holy places today where such unholy events are taking place. Can you imagine the turmoil of parents whose youngsters are involved in activities of war when they should be preparing themselves for a productive life? Is there life on hold for additional generations? Maybe they only remember fragments of ordinary life. Maybe some have known nothing but a life as insecure and bleak as those in our country who are caught in generations of drug abuse or economic depravity or unaffordable medical care. Is this a form of the discord of which Jesus spoke that will divide families? If Jesus meant to raise many questions about how we live our lives with this parable, he has succeeded.

---

1. Copyright held by the author. First published in Brauninger, *Holy E-Mail* (Lima, Ohio: CSS Publishing Company, Inc., 2001).

Parable 11

Places Of Honor

Luke 14:1, 7-14

---

1. Text

On one occasion when Jesus was going to the house of a leader of the Pharisees to eat a meal on the sabbath, they were watching him closely.

[7] When he noticed how the guests chose the places of honor, he told them a parable. [8] "When you are invited by someone to a wedding banquet, do not sit down at the place of honor, in case someone more distinguished than you has been invited by your host; [9] and the host who invited both of you may come and say to you, 'Give this person your place,' and then in disgrace you would start to take the lowest place. [10] But when you are invited, go and sit down at the lowest place, so that when your host comes, he may say to you, 'Friend, move up higher'; then you will be honored in the presence of all who sit at the table with you. [11] For all who exalt themselves will be humbled, and those who humble themselves will be exalted."

[12] He said also to the one who had invited him, "When you give a luncheon or a dinner, do not invite your friends or your brothers or your relatives or rich neighbors, in case they may invite you in return, and you would be repaid. [13] But when you give a banquet, invite the poor, the crippled, the lame, and the blind. [14] And you will be blessed, because they cannot repay you, for you will be repaid at the resurrection of the righteous."

131

2. What's Happening?

First Point Of Action

When Jesus was going to eat on the sabbath at the house of a Pharisee, he was watched closely.

Second Point Of Action

Jesus notices that the guests chose the places of honor. He tells them a parable. He said if you are invited to a wedding banquet, avoid the disgrace of sitting in the place of honor only to find that someone more distinguished than you arrives and your host must ask you to move.

Third Point Of Action

Rather, take the lowest place so your host tells you to move to the highest so your friends can enjoy your company.

Fourth Point Of Action

Jesus concludes with the wisdom saying, "For all who exalt themselves will be humbled, and those who humble themselves will be exalted."

Fifth Point Of Action

Jesus turns to his host and tells him when he gives a luncheon or a dinner, not to invite those who can repay the invitations — friends, relatives, or rich neighbors, but rather to invite those who cannot repay him — the poor, the crippled, the lame, and the blind.

Sixth Point Of Action

Jesus tells the host he will be blessed. The host will be repaid at the resurrection of the righteous.

3. Spadework

Blessed

Of the 221 "blessed" references, 38 occur in Genesis, 22 in Psalms, and 34 in the Gospels. Of those, nine are in Matthew, four in Mark, eighteen in Luke, and three in John.

The Hebrew beatitudes for everyday life read:

> *[I]f you obey your God,*
> *Blessed shall you be in the city, and blessed shall you*
> *   be in the field.*
> *Blessed shall be the fruit of your womb, the fruit of*
> *   your ground, and the fruit of your livestock, both*
> *   the increase of your cattle and the issue of your*
> *   flock.*
> *Blessed shall be your basket and your kneading bowl.*
> *Blessed shall you be when you come in, and blessed*
> *   shall you be when you go out.*
> > — Deuteronomy 28:3-6

However, for the disobedient the "cursed's" begin. (See Genesis 3:14-19.) The New Testament Beatitudes read:

> *Blessed are the poor in spirit, for theirs is the kingdom*
> *   of heaven.*
> *Blessed are those who mourn, for they will be comforted.*
> *Blessed are the meek, for they will inherit the earth.*
> *Blessed are those who hunger and thirst for righteous-*
> *   ness, for they will be filled.*
> *Blessed are the merciful, for they will receive mercy.*
> *Blessed are the pure in heart, for they will see God.*
> *Blessed are the peacemakers, for they will be called*
> *   children of God.*
> *Blessed are those who are persecuted for righteous-*
> *   ness' sake, for theirs is the kingdom of heaven.*
> *Blessed are you when people revile you and persecute*
> *   you and utter all kinds of evil against you falsely*
> *   on my account.*
> > — Matthew 5:3-11 and Luke 6:20-22

Next follow the "woe's." (See only Luke 6:24-26.)

One "blessed the Lord" (Genesis 24:48), was "blessed by the Lord" (Genesis 9:26), said, "Blessed be the [Lord] [God]" (Genesis 14:20 and 24:27), and is "the blessed of the Lord" (Genesis 26:28-29).

Sometimes the blessing is with an action: From the seed Isaac planted he "reaped a hundredfold. The Lord blessed him" (Genesis 26:12) and "Be fruitful and multiply" (Genesis 1:22, 1:28, and 9:1). See also Isaiah 51:2.

Sometimes the blessing is with words: "[Israel] blessed Joseph, and said, 'The God before whom my ancestors Abraham and Isaac walked, the God who has been my shepherd all my life to this day, the angel who has redeemed me from all harm, bless the boys; and in them let my name be perpetuated, and the name of my ancestors Abraham and Isaac; and let them grow into a multitude on the earth' " (Genesis 48:15-16).

Blessing is multi-directional. God blesses, people bless, and people are blessed: " 'Blessed be the Lord, the God of Israel, from everlasting to everlasting.' Then all the people said 'Amen!' and praised the Lord" (1 Chronicles 16:36 as quoted from Psalm 106:48). Isaac blessed Esau, thinking he was Jacob, while acknowledging " 'the smell of a field that the Lord has blessed' " (Genesis 27:27). "Saul said, 'May you be blessed by the Lord for showing me compassion!' " (1 Samuel 23:21).

The blessing is a hope for well-being, like offering one the shalom of God. "Surely the Lord your God has blessed you in all your undertakings; he knows your going through this great wilderness. These forty years the Lord your God has been with you; you have lacked nothing" (Deuteronomy 2:7).

Blessing is a way of saying thanks: "Then the women said to Naomi, 'Blessed be the Lord, who has not left you this day without next-of-kin; and may his name be renowned in Israel!' " (Ruth 4:14). God blesses the generous who share their bread with the poor (Proverbs 22:9) as does God bless "those who trust in the Lord, whose trust is the Lord" (Jeremiah 17:7).

Overflowing with "blessed," the Psalmist sings that "blessed" is a good state of being: "[B]lessed be [the Lord] [God]" (18:46, 28:6, 31:21, 41:13, 66:20, 72:18, 72:19, 78:19, 89:52, 113:2, 118:26, 124:6, 135:21, and 144:1).

How better to pay tribute to God than to bless God? "Awesome is God in his sanctuary, / the God of Israel; / he gives power and strength to his people. / Blessed be God!" (Psalm 68:35) and "Blessed are you, O Lord; / teach me your statutes" (Psalm 119:12).

The circle of blessings continues in the New Testament. When Elizabeth learned about Mary's pregnancy, she said, "Blessed are you among women, and blessed is the fruit of your womb." (See Luke 1:42 and 1:45.) Simeon took the child Jesus in his arms at the temple and blessed him. (See Luke 2:34.)

We hear a frustrated Jesus sigh to his disciples, "And blessed is anyone who takes no offense at me" (Matthew 11:6 and Luke 7:23). Jesus blesses Simon Peter for acknowledging that Jesus is "the Messiah, the Son of the living God" because "flesh and blood has not revealed this to you, but my Father in heaven" (Matthew 16:16, 17). He tells Thomas, "Have you believed because you have seen me? Blessed are those who have not seen and yet have come to believe" (John 20:29). He blesses the loaves and fish (Matthew 14:19 and Mark 6:41), the children (Mark 10:16), and before his ascension, the disciples (Luke 24:50).

On Palm Sunday, crowds wending ahead of Jesus shouted, "Hosanna to the Son of David! Blessed is the one who comes in the name of the Lord! Hosanna in the highest heaven!" (Matthew 21:9). See also Mark 11:9.

"For I tell you, you will not see me again until you say, 'Blessed is the one who comes in the name of the Lord' " (Matthew 23:39). Those who are blessed by God will " 'inherit the kingdom prepared for you from the foundation of the world' " (Matthew 25:34). In John, Jesus says we are blessed if we act upon knowing that "servants are not greater than their master, nor are messengers greater than the one who sent them" (John 13:17). He says, "Blessed is that slave whom his master will find at work when he arrives" (Matthew 24:46).

Exalted

To exalt is to elevate in rank, character, or status. Further, to exalt is to praise, glorify, or honor, to sing the praises of. Self-inflated exaltation is false. Scripture generally reads the passive "exalted (by)" unless God exalts God. Twenty-two of the seventy instances of "exalted" are from Psalms.

We cannot exalt ourselves; but God can: " 'Now I will arise,' says the Lord, 'now I will lift myself up; now I will be exalted' " (Isaiah 33:10). See also Psalm 46:10. We can, however, exalt God: "Yours, O Lord, are the greatness, the power, the glory, the victory, and the majesty; for all that is in the heavens and on the earth is yours; yours is the kingdom, O Lord, and you are exalted as head above all" (1 Chronicles 29:11). See also 2 Samuel 22:47, 1 Chronicles 29:11, Job 36:22, and Psalm 21:13.

We or ours are exalted by God: "See, my servant shall prosper; he shall be exalted and lifted up, and shall be very high" (Isaiah 52:13). A kingdom is exalted (Numbers 24:7, 2 Samuel 5:12, and 1 Chronicles 14:2). A house is exalted (1 Kings 8:13 and 2 Chronicles 6:2 and 7:21). A person is exalted (Leviticus 21:10, Joshua 4:14, 2 Samuel 22:49 and 23:1, 1 Kings 14:7 and 16:2, 1 Chronicles 29:11 and 29:25, and 2 Chronicles 32:23). "Your name" is exalted (Nehemiah 9:5). "[The mighty] are exalted a little while" (Job 24:24a). Some exalt themselves" (1 Kings 1:5).

Honor(s)

Half of the sixteen occurrences of "honor" in the Gospels refer to honoring one's father and mother. "Honor" appears 126 times in the Bible. God gave to Solomon riches, possessions, and honor because he had not asked for them but asked rather for wisdom and knowledge for himself. (See 1 Kings 3:13 and 2 Chronicles 1:11-12.)

The Psalmist is clear that honor is a gift from an honorable God: "Whoever serves me must follow me, and where I am, there will my servant be also. Whoever serves me, the Father will honor" (John 12:26); "Bless the Lord, O my soul. / O Lord my God, you are very great. / You are clothed with honor and majesty" (Psalm 104:1); "Full of honor and majesty is his work / and his righteousness endures forever" (Psalm 111:3); "[W]hat are human beings that you are mindful of them, / mortals that you care for them? / Yet you have made them a little lower than God, / and crowned them with glory and honor" (Psalm 8:4-5); and "On God rests my deliverance and my honor; / my mighty rock, my refuge is in God" (Psalm 62:7).

Honor is the result of living the right way: "For the Lord God is a sun and shield; / he bestows favor and honor. / No good thing does the Lord withhold / from those who walk uprightly" (Psalm 84:11). "Those who love me, I will deliver; / I will protect those who know my name. / When they call to me, I will answer them; / I will be with them in trouble, / I will rescue them and honor them" (Psalm 91:14-15). See also Psalm 112:9.

According to Proverbs, wisdom merits honor (Proverbs 3:35). "A person's pride will bring humiliation, / but one who is lowly in spirit will obtain honor" (Proverbs 29:23). Humility is a prerequisite (Proverbs 15:33, 18:12, and 22:4) as are righteousness and kindness (Proverbs 21:21). "It is not good to eat much honey, / or to seek honor on top of honor" (Proverbs 25:27).

On the other hand, the insincerity of honoring God with the lips "while their hearts are far from [God] and their worship of [God] is a human commandment learned by rote" yields unfavorable results. (See Isaiah 29:13ff, Matthew 15:8, and Mark 7:6.) Honor is to be given, not demanded: "Woe to you Pharisees! For you love to have the seat of honor in the synagogues and to be greeted with respect in the marketplaces" (Luke 11:43). Recognition that honor is due to an individual may be discerned only from the perspective of distance. (See Matthew 13:57 and Mark 6:4.)

(To Be) Honored

The invited guest in the present parable, who sits at the lowest place, "will be honored" by the host who then invites the guest to "move up higher." Among the other twenty occasions of "honored" are the following: Ahimelech spoke of the faithful servant David, the king's son-in-law, as honored in the king's house. (See 1 Samuel 22:14.) The honored "heed reproof" (Proverbs 13:18). "[A]nyone who takes care of a master will be honored" (Proverbs 27:18).

Host (s)

One meaning of host is a very large or indefinite number, a multitude. The relevant definition here, however, is one who hosts or provides hospitality in an official or social capacity. It also is of interest that while there are biblical instances of gracious hospitality, such

137

as Abraham's when God appeared as three men by the oaks of Mamre (Genesis 18:1ff) or the father's hospitality when the prodigal son returned home (Luke 15ff), words such as "hosting" and "hospitality" are minimal in the biblical lexicon.

Direct hospitality talk appears only in the Epistles: "Contribute to the needs of the saints; extend hospitality to strangers" (Romans 12:13); "Do not neglect to show hospitality to strangers, for by doing that some have entertained angels without knowing it" (Hebrews 13:2); and "Be hospitable to one another without complaining" (1 Peter 4:9). See also 1 Timothy 3:2 and 5:10 and Titus 1:8. The 229 occurrences of "hosts" appear as a descriptive of God with the exception of Luke 14:8 and one reference to "a host of peoples" (Ezekiel 23:24).

Humility

See Two Men At Prayer, Parable 18, Cycle C.

Place Of Honor

In addition to the present phrase, similar words appear in six additional instances: "[God] raises up the poor from the dust; he lifts the needy from the ash heap, to make them sit with princes and inherit *a seat of honor.* For the pillars of the earth are the Lord's, and on them he has set the world" (1 Samuel 2:8).

Christ scorns the religious leaders of his day for taking "*the best seats* in the synagogues and *places of honor* at banquets!" (Mark 12:39). See also Luke 11:43 and 20:46.

Resurrection

All 34 references to "resurrection" appear in the New Testament. Note the generosity of spirit in the Acts reference to "the resurrection of the righteous": "I have a hope in God — a hope that they themselves also accept — that there will be a resurrection of both the righteous and the unrighteous. Therefore I do my best always to have a clear conscience toward God and all people" (Acts 24:15-16).

Resurrection appears as part of a phrase: One finds "resurrection of the dead" in Matthew 22:31; Acts 4:2, 23:6, and 24:21; 1

Corinthians 15:21 and 15:42; and Hebrews 6:2. "In the resurrection from the dead" occurs in Luke 20:35 and Romans 1:4. "In the resurrection" appears in Matthew 22:28 and 22:30; and Luke 20:33. Luke 20:36 reads, "at the resurrection." "Christ's resurrection" occurs in Acts 1:22, 2:31, and 4:33; and in 1 Peter 1:3 and 3:21. John speaks of "the resurrection of life" and "the resurrection of condemnation." "Do not be astonished at this; for the hour is coming when all who are in their graves will hear his voice and will come out — those who have done good, to the resurrection of life, and those who have done evil, to the resurrection of condemnation" (John 5:28-29). Several New Testament writers mention the argument of belief in resurrection. See Matthew 22:23, Mark 12:18, Luke 20:27, Acts 17:32 and 23:8, and 1 Corinthians 15:12.

(The) Righteous
Of the 140 "the righteous" references, 37 appear in the Psalms. God "watches over the way of the righteous ..." (Psalm 1:6). God blesses the righteous and covers "them with favor as with a shield" (Psalm 5:12). "The eyes of the Lord are on the righteous, and his ears are open to their cry" (Psalm 34:15). God hears when the righteous cry for help "and rescues them from all their troubles" (Psalm 34:17).

Still, the way of the righteous is not automatic bliss: "[God] makes his sun rise on the evil and on the good, and sends rain on the righteous and on the unrighteous" (Matthew 5:45). See also Psalm 11:5.

Both the Psalmist and the writer of Proverbs are given to couplets comparing the righteous to the wicked: "The wicked borrow, and do not pay back, but the righteous are generous and keep giving" (Psalm 37:21). See also Psalm 37:16-17.

Proverbs 10 through 15, 21, 28, and 29 present a series of comparisons between the righteous and the wicked: "Blessings are on the head of the righteous, but the mouth of the wicked conceals violence. The memory of the righteous is a blessing, but the name of the wicked will rot" (Proverbs 10:6-7). "When justice is done, it is a joy to the righteous, but dismay to evildoers" (Proverbs 21:15).

"Then once more you shall see the difference between the righteous and the wicked, between one who serves God and one who does not serve him" (Malachi 3:18).

Are the righteous always the underdogs? "[T]he Lord opens the eyes of the blind. / The Lord lifts up those who are bowed down; / the Lord loves the righteous" (Psalm 146:8). "People will say, / 'Surely there is a reward for the righteous; / surely there is a God who judges on earth' " (Psalm 58:11).

The righteous are an aware, faithful, and persevering lot: "Yet the righteous hold to their way, and they that have clean hands grow stronger and stronger" (Job 17:9). See also Proverbs 9:9 and Psalm 37:30. "Look at the proud! Their spirit is not right in them, but the righteous live by their faith" (Habakkuk 2:4). See also Luke 1:17 and 5:32.

4. Parallel Scripture

Banquets

"[D]o not invite your friends or your brothers or your relatives or rich neighbors ... invite the poor, the crippled, the lame, and the blind" (Luke 14:12, 13). Compare with guest lists of other biblical banquets:

At the other wedding banquet, the invited guests could not be bothered to come, so the host "said to his slaves, 'The wedding is ready, but those invited were not worthy. Go therefore into the main streets, and invite everyone you find to the wedding banquet.' Those slaves went out into the streets and gathered all whom they found, both good and bad; so the wedding hall was filled with guests" (Matthew 22:8-10).

In Esther three banquets were given: the king's "for all the people present in the citadel of Susa, both great and small" (Esther 1:5); the queen's for the women (see Esther 1:9); and the king's "for all his officials and ministers" (Esther 2:18). Herod gave a banquet "for his courtiers and officers and for the leaders of Galilee" (Mark 6:21). "Then Levi gave a great banquet for him in his house; and there was a large crowd of tax collectors and others sitting at the table with them" (Luke 5:29).

140

Exalted Humility

In the present parable, Jesus says, "For all who exalt themselves will be humbled, *and* those who humble themselves will be exalted" (Luke 14:11). In the parable of Two Men At Prayer (Cycle C, Parable 18), Jesus says, "... for all who exalt themselves will be humbled, *but* all who humble themselves will be exalted" (see Luke 18:9-14). In Matthew, Jesus says, "The greatest among you will be your servant. All who exalt themselves will be humbled, *and* all who humble themselves will be exalted" (Matthew 23:11-12).

Also in Matthew, Jesus says, "Whoever becomes humble like this child is the greatest in the kingdom of heaven" (Matthew 18:4). Capernaum will not be exalted but will be brought down. (See Matthew 11:23 and Luke 10:15.)

5. Chat Room

Michelle: We had a clergy couple in our rural church who were both awarded honorary doctorate degrees after serving for a number of years. Unlike academic degrees earned after book study, this degree was a blessing, a gift for life work. It was earned, literally at times, in the field. Completely surprised, each minister quietly credited the other, saying their seminary must have felt it could not award one without the other. It took a bit before their reserve gave way to full-blown delight. Still, they continued to use the "Reverend" title, lest "Doctor" seem ostentatious to farm folk.

Francisco: This is the surprise of blessing. God notices. This is being taken unawares with the invitation to sit in the honored seat.

Gary: To our surprise, we do have a positive effect upon others without design. To our surprise, others observe and reflect upon our efforts. To our surprise, our enjoyable and demanding work is acknowledged when our minds are turned away from recompense or reward and least expect it.

Francisco: Blessing is good. It occurs to me that perhaps blessing strikes when God observes that a part of our soul needs tending. Our tender and tending God says, "Now is the time."

Gary: The soul also needs tending when self-aggrandizement happens. We should not have to seek recognition. It will come when it is appropriate.

Michelle: The part of the soul that needs the ego trip suffers its own hunger. I can always tell when the domineering, spiritually abusive partner of a woman I know is on the rampage again. She also becomes obnoxious by playing the one-upmanship game. She demands to be right. She must have the last word. She —

Francisco: She needs a blessing. She is fighting for emotional survival. She is starving for worth. Her opinion needs to count. Nobody recognizes her validity, so she attempts to claim one for herself. She needs a blessing.

Gary: Our conversation has awakened two phrases in my mind: The distinguished disgrace of taking the humble seat if by nature you are a proud person. Exalted humility and what you do with it if you are a naturally humble person.

Francisco: Distinguished disgrace and exalted humility, those are ironic contradictions for you. It invites me to think about the inner continuum that ranges within each of us from the need for affirmation to the need to affirm others.

Michelle: I suppose somewhere on that continuum is the variable line where inner discontent and inner ease meet. My thoughts go to how the world around us perceives us, and how that differs from how we view ourselves.

Francisco: I would add another phrase to ponder — graciousness in perceiving what is blessing. What are the voices from whom we need to hear blessing? Those around us who mean something to us? That valid affirmation from our own generosity of spirit? The voice of our Creator that sees beyond all sorts of artificial position to show itself in any number of ways as blessing?

Michelle: Thanks to a gracious and faithful God, modern day invitations to the place of honor come when you least expect them.

Parable 12

Counting The Cost

Luke 14:25-33

---

1. Text

Now large crowds were traveling with him; and he turned and said to them, [26] "Whoever comes to me and does not hate father and mother, wife and children, brothers and sisters, yes, and even life itself, cannot be my disciple. [27] Whoever does not carry the cross and follow me cannot be my disciple. [28] For which of you, intending to build a tower, does not first sit down and estimate the cost, to see whether he has enough to complete it? [29] Otherwise, when he has laid a foundation and is not able to finish, all who see it will begin to ridicule him, [30] saying, 'This fellow began to build and was not able to finish.' [31] Or what king, going out to wage war against another king, will not sit down first and consider whether he is able with ten thousand to oppose the one who comes against him with twenty thousand? [32] If he cannot, then, while the other is still far away, he sends a delegation and asks for the terms of peace. [33] So therefore, none of you can become my disciple if you do not give up all your possessions."

2. What's Happening?

First Point Of Action

Jesus addresses the men in the large crowds traveling with him with two "whoever's."

Second Point Of Action

First, he tells them whoever comes to him and does not hate father, mother, wife, children, sisters, and even life itself cannot be his disciple.

Third Point Of Action

Second, he tells them whoever does not carry the cross and follow him cannot be his disciple.

Fourth Point Of Action

First, Jesus uses the analogy of counting the cost, that is, estimating to determine whether one has enough funds to complete a tower before beginning to build it. Otherwise, the builder will be ridiculed by all who see that he has laid a foundation and is unable to complete it.

Fifth Point Of Action

Second, Jesus uses the analogy of a king considering before going out to wage war against another king whether he is able with 10,000 fighters to oppose the one who comes against him with 20,000. If he cannot, while the other is still far away, he sends a delegation and asks for the terms of peace.

Sixth Point Of Action

Jesus concludes with the "So therefore," no one can become his disciple without giving up all possessions.

3. Spadework

Carry The Cross

Used on 108 occasions, "carry" appears in the physical way of carrying grain, choice fruits, sacks, bags, money, my bones, the ark, the table, the altar, the bull, the ashes, your kinsmen, the carcass, the things of the tent of the meeting, the tabernacle, seed, twelve stones, seven trumpets of rams' horns, plunder, and the cross.

"Carry" also appears in an intangible way as "carry out his fierce wrath" (1 Samuel 28:18), "carry the good news" (1 Samuel

31:9 and 1 Chronicles 10:9), "carry out exactly the decision" (Deuteronomy 10:8), "carry on his work" (Judges 16:8), "carry tidings" (2 Samuel 18:19), "carry him to his mother" (2 Kings 4:19), "carry out a plan" (Isaiah 30:1), "carry out all my purpose" (Isaiah 44:28), "carry my shame" (2 Samuel 13:13), "carry their own loads" (Galatians 6:5), and the cross (Luke 9:23).

Further, "carry" takes on the tender dimension in the relationship of God and the human family:

"He will feed his flock like a shepherd; he will gather the lambs in his arms, and carry them in his bosom, and gently lead the mother sheep" (Isaiah 40:11);

"Listen to me, O house of Jacob, all the remnant of the house of Israel, who have been borne by me from your birth, carried from the womb; even to your old age I am he, even when you turn gray I will carry you. I have made, and I will bear; I will carry and will save" (Isaiah 46:3-4);

"O save your people, and bless your heritage; / be their shepherd, and carry them forever" (Psalm 28:9); and

"[A]nd in the wilderness, where you saw how the Lord your God carried you, just as one carries a child, all the way that you traveled until you reached this place" (Deuteronomy 1:31).

Choice (Choose)

Except for two New Testament references, "choice" is a word of Hebrew Scripture with 77 occurrences: choice flour, choice gifts, fruits, meal, votive gifts, city, sheep, gold, silver, vines, vessel, bones, garments, portion of the land, sacrifices, choice sacrifices, and make no choice at all.

Make a choice, take your choice: When the people of Benjamin and Levi were excluded from the census, a displeased God offered David three choices of punishment, "Now decide what answer I shall return to the one who sent me" (1 Chronicles 21:11-12).

While "choose" occurs 65 times in the Bible, "chosen" occurs 107 times. Is anything else quite as affirming as this statement of God's choice? "Here is my servant, whom I uphold, my chosen, in whom my soul delights; I have put my spirit upon him; he will bring forth justice to the nations" (Isaiah 42:1).

147

From the beginning, God chooses: "No, for I have chosen him, that he may charge his children and his household after him to keep the way of the Lord by doing righteousness and justice; so that the Lord may bring about for Abraham what he has promised him" (Genesis 18:19) and "For you are a people holy to the Lord your God; the Lord your God has chosen you out of all the peoples on earth to be his people, his treasured possession" (Deuteronomy 14:2). See also Joshua 24:22.

Consider the interplay of choosing and having been chosen. In all three versions of Jesus' healing of the leper, the leper confronts Jesus with these words, "Lord, if you choose, you can make me clean," and Jesus responds, "I do choose" (Matthew 8:2-3, Mark 1:40-41, and Luke 5:12-13).

God has a hand in our choices: "I call heaven and earth to witness against you today that I have set before you life and death, blessings and curses. Choose life so that you and your descendants may live" (Deuteronomy 30:19); "Let us choose what is right; let us determine among ourselves what is good" (Job 34:4); "Who are they that fear the Lord? / He will teach them the way that they should choose" (Psalm 25:12); and "You did not choose me but I chose you. And I appointed you to go and bear fruit, fruit that will last, so that the Father will give you whatever you ask him in my name" (John 15:16). (For "Chose [Chosen]," see also The Uncaring Judge, Parable17, Cycle C.)

[The] Cost

God sets before us the unlikely juxtaposition of "the cost and joy of discipleship."[1] The cost can be severe, the cost of a life: "Moses said, 'Today you have ordained yourselves for the service of the Lord, each one at the cost of a son or a brother, and so have brought a blessing on yourselves this day' " (see Exodus 32:27-29). " 'At the cost of his firstborn he shall lay its foundation, and at the cost of his youngest he shall set up its gates!' " (Joshua 6:26). See also Numbers 16:38, 1 Kings 16:34, and 1 Chronicles 12:19.

What is the price? "Truly, no ransom avails for one's life, / there is no price one can give to God for it" (Psalm 49:7). "Then was fulfilled what had been spoken through the prophet Jeremiah,

'And they took the thirty pieces of silver, the price of the one on whom a price had been set, on whom some of the people of Israel had set a price' " (Matthew 27:9). "For you were bought with a price; therefore glorify God in your body" (1 Corinthians 6:20) and "You were bought with a price; do not become slaves of human masters" (1 Corinthians 7:23).

Cross

"Cross" carries the intertwined meanings from cross into, cross to, and cross over to crossing the bridge from one way of life to another to being cross to cross-examination. In addition to the present parable, Jesus refers to the cross four other times before the Crucifixion: "[A]nd whoever does not take up the cross and follow me is not worthy of me" (Matthew 10:38) and "Then he said to them all, 'If any want to become my followers, let them deny themselves and take up their cross daily and follow me' " (Luke 9:23). See also Matthew 16:24 and Mark 8:34.

Simon of Cyrene was compelled to carry the cross. (See Mark 15:21; Matthew 27:32, 27:40, and 27:42; Mark 15:30 and 15:32; Luke 23:26; and John 19:19, 19:25, and 19:31.) Jesus voluntarily carried the cross: "[A]nd carrying the cross by himself, he went out to what is called The Place of the Skull, which in Hebrew is called Golgotha" (John 19:17).

Disciple

Of the 21 references to "disciple," all in the New Testament, three are from Matthew, four from Luke, and nine from John. The two instances of "my [Jesus'] disciple" occur in the present parable. Two versions of the same saying are the only explicit definition of a disciple: "A disciple is not above the teacher, but everyone who is fully qualified will be like the teacher" (Luke 6:40). See also Matthew 10:24.

"A disciple" occurs twice, as a specific identifier naming Joseph of Arimathea as *a disciple* of Jesus (Matthew 27:57) and as a general reference to the disciples. (See Matthew 10:42.) *"The disciple* whom Jesus loved" occurs in John 19:26 and 21:20. The "this disciple" in John 21:23 refers to the disciple whom Jesus loved.

149

John or a later editor refers to the writer "*the disciple who* is testifying to these things and has written them, and we know that his testimony is true" (John 21:24).

"Disciples" occurs 129 times: Matthew, 58; Mark, 39; Luke, 31; and John, fifteen, with 21 appearances in Acts but none in the letters. "Discipleship" does not appear in the Bible.

Hate

To "hate father and mother, wife and children, brothers and sisters, yes, and even life itself" (Luke 14:26) is the opposite of what one would expect from Jesus. God or family? Does Jesus use "hate" for dramatic effect? Even the Beatitudes are not exempt: "Blessed are you when people hate you, and when they exclude you, revile you, and defame you on account of the Son of Man" (Luke 6:22).

Hate is neither casual nor lukewarm. A beginning definition of "hate" includes "those from whom you turned in disgust" (Ezekiel 23:28), "despise" and "take no delight in" (Amos 5:21), and "abhor" (Amos 6:8). Nevertheless, there is "... a time to love, and a time to hate; a time for war, and a time for peace" (Ecclesiastes 3:8).

Proverbs lists "six things that the Lord hates, seven that are an abomination to him" (Proverbs 6:16). The seventh is "one who sows discord in a family" (Proverbs 6:19).

What about the relatives? "Your own people who hate you and reject you for my name's sake have said, 'Let the Lord be glorified, so that we may see your joy'; but it is they who shall be put to shame" (Isaiah 66:5b) and "My heritage has become to me like a lion in the forest; she has lifted up her voice against me — therefore I hate her" (Jeremiah 12:8).

On the other hand, see Malachi 2:16, as well as writings from 1 John: "Whoever says, 'I am in the light,' while hating a brother or sister, is still in the darkness. Whoever loves a brother or sister lives in the light, and in such a person there is no cause for stumbling" (1 John 2:9-10). See also 1 John 3:15 and 1 John 4:20. Is this the later writer's response to the present parable?

No wonder the philosopher, who has contemplated the ways of "business that is done on earth ... and all the work of God," concludes "that no one can find out what is happening under the sun. However much they may toil in seeking, they will not find it out; even though those who are wise claim to know, they cannot find it out. All this I laid to heart, examining it all, how the righteous and the wise and their deeds are in the hand of God; whether it is love or hate one does not know. Everything that confronts them is vanity, since the same fate comes to all...." (See Ecclesiastes 8:16—9:2.)

"Hate" occurs 91 times, 31 of which are in Psalms. In the Gospels, it occurs three times in Matthew and John and five times in Luke. Of particular interest are the following passages: "You shall not hate in your heart anyone of your kin" (Leviticus 19:17a) and "For no one ever hates his own body, but he nourishes and tenderly cares for it, just as Christ does for the church" (Ephesians 5:29).

In addition to the present parable, two other passages refer to hating one's own life. "To be a partner of a thief is to hate one's own life; one hears the victim's curse, but discloses nothing" (Proverbs 29:24) and "Those who love their life lose it, and those who hate their life in this world will keep it for eternal life" (John 12:25).

"If the world hates you, be aware that it hated me before it hated you. If you belonged to the world, the world would love you as its own. Because you do not belong to the world, but I have chosen you out of the world — therefore the world hates you" (John 15:18-19).

Possess(es)

"Possess" appears 62 times. Most of the time God is the giver of these possessions and the possession is the result of design or plan. God gave "land" (Genesis 15:7, Exodus 23:30, Leviticus 20:24, Numbers 14:24 and 33:53, Deuteronomy 5:31, 5:33, 19:2, 19:14, 21:1, 23:20, 28:21, 28:63, 30:5, 30:16, 30:18, 31:13, and 32:47; 1 Chronicles 28:8; Ezra 9:11; and Amos 2:10).

Part of a blessing was to "possess the gate of their enemies" (Genesis 22:17). Some persons possessed "an inheritance" (Numbers 27:7, 27:11, 35:2, and 36:8; Deuteronomy 25:19 and 26:1;

Psalm 25:13; and Isaiah 34:17 and 54:3). Others possessed "God-given wisdom" (Ezra 7:25 and Psalm 69:35) or "the kingdom forever" (Daniel 7:18).

The following passages indicate their participation and the additional action of taking for themselves force beyond merely accepting the land that God is giving: "[G]o in to take possession of the land that the Lord your God gives you to possess" (Joshua 1:11); "[C]lear [the hill land] and possess it" (Joshua 17:18); and "[Y]ou shall possess their land as the Lord your God promised you" (Joshua 23:5). See also Nehemiah 9:11 and 9:23.

The possession comes with the responsibility of a connection with God: "But whoever takes refuge in me shall possess the land and inherit my holy mountain" (Isaiah 57:13) and "Your people shall all be righteous; they shall possess the land forever. They are the shoot that I planted, the work of my hands, so that I might be glorified" (Isaiah 60:21).

Hebrew Scripture is a story of possession as the domination of other people: "The house of Israel will possess the nations as male and female slaves in the Lord's land" (Isaiah 14:2); "I will lead people upon you — my people Israel — and they shall possess you, and you shall be their inheritance. No longer shall you bereave them of children" (Ezekiel 36:12); and "The powerful possess the land, and the favored live in it" (Job 22:8).

This passage suggests a reluctance to take the land: "[The five land scouts reported to their kinsfolk], 'Come, let us go up against them; for we have seen the land, and it is very good. Will you do nothing? Do not be slow to go, but enter in and possess the land' " (Judges 18:9).

By giving up "all your possessions," might Jesus mean that nothing else but following him must be in first place or dominate us? In the level of soul, we must be single-minded. (See "Possessions" in Section Four.) In the Gospels, many were "possessed by demons." See Matthew 8:16, Mark 1:32 and 1:18, and Luke 8:36. When one's possessions get out of hand, they become as demons. (See also The Rich Fool, Parable 8, Cycle C.)

Paul reminded the Corinthian Christians that servants of God are treated "as sorrowful, yet always rejoicing; as poor, yet making many rich; as having nothing, and yet possessing everything" (2 Corinthians 6:10).

4. Parallel Scripture

Tone Of The Parable

The present parable is laid out negatively: "Whoever does not carry the cross and follow me cannot be my disciple" (Luke 14:27). Earlier, Luke reports that "Jesus said to them all, 'If any want to become my followers, let them deny themselves and take up their cross daily and follow me'" (Luke 9:23). Mark uses the same quotation, prefacing it with "He called the crowd with his disciples, and said to them" (Mark 8:34). Also using this quotation, Matthew prefaces with "Then Jesus told his disciples" (Matthew 16:24).

Whoever

The first "Whoever" of the present parable, "Whoever comes to me and does not hate father and mother, wife and children, brothers and sisters, yes, and even life itself, cannot be my disciple" (Luke 14:26), has a parallel in Matthew. Where Luke says, "cannot be my disciple," Matthew says, "is not worthy of me" (Matthew 10:37). Here, Matthew uses "love ... more than me" in the first two of the three "Whoever's." Matthew says nothing of wife and children or brothers and sisters or even life itself. Rather, he says, "father or mother" and "son or daughter" (Matthew 10:37).

Matthew's third "Whoever" corresponds to Luke's second. Matthew says, "does not take up the cross" (Matthew 10:38) and "take up their cross" (Matthew 16:24), where Luke says, "does not carry the cross." Luke says, "cannot be my disciple," and Matthew says, "is not worthy of me" (Matthew 10:38).

Possessions

"So therefore, none of you can become my disciple if you do not give up all your possessions" (Luke 14:33). Earlier, the writer of Luke records, "Sell your possessions, and give alms" (Luke 12:33). Prefacing his words with "Jesus said to him," Matthew says, "If you wish to be perfect" and "sell your possessions." He also says to "give the money to the poor" and finally, "then come, follow me" (Matthew 19:21). Mark's version is identical to Matthew's except for the preface, "Jesus, looking at him, loved him and said, 'You lack one thing' " (Mark 10:21). The man was unidentified in either Matthew or Mark's telling.

5. Chat Room

Chat A
Edna: If you cannot do it then do something else. Find an alternative. Wait until you are at a different point in your life where you can make the commitment with your whole heart. Just do not do it unless you are sure.

Meta: I want this decision to be right. I'm no fool, and I want to let down no one.

Edna: There is no condemnation or ridicule in saying no. The problem lies in making all the commitments with all the other opportunities that it would eliminate or in the waste of the whole thing if you discover you have miscalculated or your heart really is not in it or you cannot pay the cost of this commitment.

Meta: Surely others will think my choice is impulsive if not irresponsible.

Edna: From the perspective of some, you will be seen as a fool if you take on this task. You may even wonder yourself.

Meta: The cost of such discipleship looms greater than the joy for me. I must be asking the wrong questions for one who might be willing to make such a commitment.

Edna: It could also be your honesty and thoroughness before making a life-changing decision. Take your time.

Chat B

Karl: I will carry this burden, and this and this, but no cross. I will sacrifice all my personal time and energy for family, but I will not desert them. Would it not be more selfish than selfless to be so dedicated to God?

And how can I hate the people I love? Hate even life itself? Whatever are you talking about, Jesus, with this hate stuff? You are the teacher of love.

Tony: For me, this hate that Christ speaks of has little to do with not loving. It has more to do with the intensity of focusing on the true cost of following Christ. Discipleship is definitely not a convenience thing.

On the other hand, I do parry the issue. What Jesus is dedicated to accomplishing transcends all else for him — possessions, lifestyle, and relationships. It is a new way of looking at things. It is an ideal to strive for.

Karl: How can I just waste all this education and training? How can I leave behind the years I have apprenticed in my craft? If only this choice could avoid being in the category of the either/or. I do not have time in my week for that kind of dedication. Can't I just follow you in my heart, Jesus, and live my regular life on the side?

Tony: For me, the conflict is the pull. The part of my soul that needs tending is the part this parable upsets so.

Karl: Sorry, I forgot you were online. What do you mean?

Tony: I have started to look at how I am living now, at how I do hate the people I love whenever I put my family second or even third by not making time for them, whenever I neglect them by not providing monetarily or emotionally.

I also have begun to think about those times I am not true to the terms of my relationships. I hate life itself when I am not true to what I was once committed to. I hate life when I ignore good self-care and fail to take preventative health measures. I hate life when I fail to preserve and conserve with good earth stewardship practices. Unless I give up those possessions that I have let possess me, I am choosing not to follow the ways of Christ.

Chat C

Elsa: After all these years, God, I am beginning to understand that what I thought was *my* choice for vocation is more than a calling.

God: "Many are called but few are chosen" (Matthew 22:14).

Elsa: It all has to do with your choosing. From the very beginning with the gifts you gave me, with my inner yearning and beckoning, with the way my life has evolved, you have been present.

God: Where was I and where am I in all of this? Right in the middle. At first, "[y]ou did not choose me but I chose you" (John 15:16a).

Elsa: Everything that has happened to me has had a reason that fit into the whole purpose of my being. When I pondered earlier why you chose me for this life, when I wondered originally why my will could not be your will, I failed to understand your role in my life. Now I do.

God: "I will teach [you] the way that [you] should choose" (Psalm 25:12).

Elsa: Thank you for waiting. And God, thank you for being patient.

---

1. From the Statement of Faith, United Church of Christ.

Parable 13

Lost And Found

Luke 15:1-10

---

1. Text

*Now all the tax collectors and sinners were coming near
to listen to him. [2] And the Pharisees and the scribes
were grumbling and saying, "This fellow welcomes sinners and eats with them."*

*[3] So he told them this parable: [4] "Which one
of you, having a hundred sheep and losing one of them,
does not leave the ninety-nine in the wilderness and go
after the one that is lost until he finds it? [5] When he
has found it, he lays it on his shoulders and rejoices.
[6] And when he comes home, he calls together his
friends and neighbors, saying to them, 'Rejoice with
me, for I have found my sheep that was lost.' [7] Just
so, I tell you, there will be more joy in heaven over one
sinner who repents than over ninety-nine righteous persons who need no repentance.*

*[8] "Or what woman having ten silver coins, if
she loses one of them, does not light a lamp, sweep the
house, and search carefully until she finds it? [9] When
she has found it, she calls together her friends and
neighbors, saying, 'Rejoice with me, for I have found
the coin that I had lost.' [10] Just so, I tell you, there is
joy in the presence of the angels of God over one sinner who repents."*

2. What's Happening?

First Point Of Action
Jesus responds to the grumbling of the Pharisees and scribes about his association with sinners and tax collectors by telling two parables.

Second Point Of Action
Jesus tells the parable of the lost sheep.

Third Point Of Action
The shepherd leaves the 99 sheep to search until finding the one lost.

Fourth Point Of Action
Upon finding the lost sheep, the shepherd gathers together friends and neighbors to celebrate.

Fifth Point Of Action
Jesus makes the "Just so" analogy with God's joy over one repentant sinner.

Sixth Point Of Action
Jesus tells the parable of the lost coin.

Seventh Point Of Action
The woman who has lost one of her ten coins lights a lamp, sweeps the floor, searching until she finds the coin.

Eighth Point Of Action
Upon finding the lost coin, the woman gathers together friends and neighbors to celebrate.

Ninth Point Of Action
Jesus again makes the "Just so" analogy with God's joy over one repentant sinner.

3. Spadework

(Leave In The) Wilderness

Upon first consideration, one wonders about the foolish dimension of risking the loss of all the sheep for the sake of trying to save one. In presenting the story with "Which one of you does not [do this]?" Jesus presumes that those he addressed took care of their treasures. Even the youngest of shepherds, David, knew enough not to leave sheep unattended. If the shepherd in the present parable cared enough to go in search of one lost sheep, he also would have provided a keeper for the rest of the flock.

When the battle broke out, David, the youngest son of an aging father, was left in charge of caring for his father's sheep. Prior to his encounter with Goliath, David left the sheep with a keeper and went back and forth between the sheep and the battleground taking food there as his father had instructed. Despite David's provision for the sheep, the family's livelihood, his oldest and perhaps jealous brother still accused him of being irresponsible. (See 1 Samuel 17.)

The issue is the same for spending money so that all members of a confirmation class, including a youth with spina bifida, will be welcome to approach the chancel to serve as acolyte. The issue is the same for removing a section of a pew so a grandmother who uses a wheelchair can sit with the rest of her family instead of in the back. The issue is the same for converting a pulpit so a minister who lives with the effects of early polio can avoid preaching from a folding chair.

Is the cost-effectiveness, the money, or the intrinsic value of each person of greatest importance? The issue is the same. Accessibility action that makes a church a welcoming church happens when that church recognizes and honors the preciousness of one among its members.

The wilderness of societal attitudes is a potentially physically dangerous and spiritually lethal place that can cause aimless circling and wandering. Wilderness can "close in on" those caught in even its subtlest forms of injustice. "Pharaoh will say of the

Israelites, 'They are wandering aimlessly in the land; the wilderness has closed in on them' " (Exodus 14:3).

Consider the impact of the geographical wilderness upon the lives of the Hebrew people that causes "wilderness" to appear 206 times in Hebrew Scripture. New Testament usage includes 33 occasions. The wilderness can be treacherous. "[God] who led you through the great and terrible wilderness, an arid wasteland with poisonous snakes and scorpions. He made water flow for you from flint rock, and fed you in the wilderness with manna that your ancestors did not know, to humble you and to test you, and in the end to do you good" (Deuteronomy 8:15-16). See also Numbers 21:5.

Like the shepherd, God enters the wilderness and is aware of our goings on: "[A]nd in the wilderness, where you saw how the Lord your God carried you, just as one carries a child, all the way that you traveled until you reached this place" (Deuteronomy 1:31). "Surely the Lord your God has blessed you in all your undertakings; he knows your going through this great wilderness" (Deuteronomy 2:7).

Whenever those with the capacity to empower one who suffers an injustice step into that wilderness, the issue that brought the suffering one into the wilderness begins to resolve. See also Deuteronomy 29:5 and 32:10.

Beyond the shepherd metaphor of Psalm 23, the following Psalm segments reflect this image of God's protective, sustaining care: "Then he led out his people like sheep, and guided them in the wilderness like a flock" (Psalm 78:52) and "He led them in safety, so that they were not afraid" (Psalm 78:53).

Lost And Found

Both singer and prophet use the lost sheep metaphor: "I have gone astray like a lost sheep; seek out your servant, / for I do not forget your commandments" (Psalm 119:176). Jeremiah suggests that the straying was intentional and caused by the shepherd rather than through the wandering of an innocent lamb: "My people have been lost sheep; their shepherds have led them astray, turning them away on the mountains; from mountain to hill they have gone, they have forgotten their fold" (Jeremiah 50:6).

160

Where, one asks, is the line between innocent wandering and cognizance of misguided leadership? "But we are not among those who shrink back and so are lost, but among those who have faith and so are saved" (Hebrew 10:39).

Should the lamb who strays and becomes lost be let go for the sake of the flock or any other reason? Ezekiel chides the "shepherds" of Israel: "You have not strengthened the weak, you have not healed the sick, you have not bound up the injured, you have not brought back the strayed, you have not sought the lost, but with force and harshness you have ruled them" (Ezekiel 34:4). In contrast, "For thus says the Lord God: I myself will search for my sheep, and will seek them out" (Ezekiel 34:11) and "I will seek the lost, and I will bring back the strayed, and I will bind up the injured, and I will strengthen the weak, but the fat and the strong I will destroy. I will feed them with justice" (Ezekiel 34:16).

Jesus continues the metaphor as his mission: "For the Son of Man came to seek out and to save the lost" (Luke 19:10). When he was approached by the Canaanite woman with the sick child, he refused her at first, "I was sent only to the lost sheep of the house of Israel" (Matthew 15:24).

Was it Christ's profound respect for all things, even leftover food from feeding the masses, that kept him focused on no one or nothing being lost? "When they were satisfied, he told his disciples, 'Gather up the fragments left over, so that nothing may be lost' " (John 6:12). "So it is not the will of your Father in heaven that one of these little ones should be lost" (Matthew 18:14).

In the Johanine prayer of Christ with God, he told God that he had kept his promise to fulfill scripture. He had protected, guarded, and kept from being lost all the disciples except the one who "was destined to be lost." (See John 17:12.)

Referring to the condition of the soul, the "lost and found" phrase appears twice in the parable of the Prodigal Sons in Luke 15. (See Cycle C, Parable 4.) Those who have been lost know its desperation, helplessness, and sense of permanence. "And I said: 'Woe is me! I am lost' " (Isaiah 6:5) and, as if thrown into a pit, "[W]ater closed over my head; I said, 'I am lost' " (Lamentations 3:54). "The fruit for which your soul longed has gone from you, and all your dainties and your splendor are lost to you, never to be found again!" (Revelation 18:14).

One wonders if the couplet parables of The Lost Sheep and The Lost Coin were designed to be inclusive, that is, the former happened to a man and the later to a woman. The quiet messages — the struggle and its resolution, losing and finding — belong to all. Everyone counts, the one lost and the one who finds.

For additional study of "lost and found," see "Seek/Find" in Cycle C, Parable 7, The Midnight Friend, and "Lose Heart" in Cycle C, Parable 17, The Uncaring Judge.

Pieces Of Silver

The woman had ten pieces of silver. Were these to have lasted her lifetime, or would she have to refrain from buying prescription drugs? Silver coins were used for larger transactions. Judas Iscariot's payment for betraying Jesus was thirty pieces of silver. This phrase occurs thirteen times in scripture. The four references to "pieces of silver" in the New Testament are in Matthew. They refer to the betrayal money.

The three biblical references to "coin" appear in the writings of Luke and Matthew. Three of the five biblical references to "coins" also are in the Synoptic Gospels. In addition to the present text, Mark 12:42 and Luke 21:2 refer to the "two small copper coins" the poor widow gave.

Rejoice

Rejoice (rejoices, rejoiced, rejoicing) and joy are familiar biblical words. Of the 362 references, 44 appear in the Gospels. Let us look at the occasions for using the word "rejoice" in the Synoptic Gospels.

For the writer of Luke, Christianity is a religion that smiles. The compassionate Luke also knows how to uplift with rejoicing. He must have contained much joy within his spirit. The first Lukan reference refers to the angel's announcement to Zechariah about the coming birth of John to Elizabeth. The attitude and response: "You will have joy and gladness, and many will rejoice at his birth" (Luke 1:14).

In the Lukan Beatitudes, those whom others hate, exclude, revile, and defame because of the Son of God are to "rejoice in that day and leap for joy" (Luke 6:23). Similarly in the Beatitudes according to Matthew, the persecuted are to "Rejoice and be glad, for your reward is great in heaven, for in the same way they persecuted the prophets who were before you" (Matthew 5:12). Luke would have us rejoice that our names are written in heaven (Luke 10:20), when the lost sheep, the lost coin and the younger prodigal son are found.

Looking at "rejoices," again in Luke with the Magnificat, Mary rejoices: "My soul magnifies the Lord, and my spirit rejoices in God my Savior" (Luke 1:46-47). Both Mary and Zechariah may well have quaked with uncertainty at the news of their unexpected babies. Their, and our, response of choice in our faith albeit conditioned by nudging from an angel is positive, rejoicing. Matthew 18:13 and Luke 15:5 use "rejoices" in reference to the lost sheep parable.

Luke is home to the one occasion of "rejoicing" in the Synoptic Gospels: "When [Jesus said it was more important to set free a woman from the bondage of her crippling than not to do so on the Sabbath], all his opponents were put to shame; and the entire crowd was rejoicing at all the wonderful things that he was doing" (Luke 13:17).

The two usages of "rejoiced" also appear in Luke: When Elizabeth gave birth, "[h]er neighbors and relatives ... rejoiced with her" (Luke 1:58) and Jesus thanked God and "rejoiced in the Holy Spirit" (Luke 10:21).

With seventeen appearances in the Synoptic Gospels, "joy" occurs six times in Matthew, once in Mark, and ten times in Luke. For Lukan references to "joy," see Luke 1:14, 1:44, 2:10, 6:23, 8:13, 10:17, 15:7, 15:10, 24:41, and 24:52. See also Matthew 2:10, 13:20, 13:44, 25:21, 25:23, and 28:8; and Mark 4:16. While from these scriptures one notices that rejoicing is both solitary and communal, in the present parables rejoicing needs a friend or seven as both finders say, "Rejoice with me."

Shoulders

Twenty of the 22 references to "shoulders" occur in Hebrew Scripture. While tossing a lamb over the shoulders offers a practical and safe way to move a lamb any distance, the phrasing of the text, "lays it *on* its shoulders," emphasizes the gentle, tender carrying of the sheep. Was this the place for protecting what is most precious? The most holy items that would go in the tabernacle were to be carried on the shoulders rather than in the wagons. (See Numbers 7:9.)

The shoulders image appears in Deuteronomy. "Of Benjamin [Moses] said: The beloved of the Lord rests in safety — the High God surrounds him all day long — the beloved rests *between* his shoulders" (Deuteronomy 33:12). See also Deuteronomy 1:31 above. The Messiah passage in Isaiah again uses shoulders as an image of having, being given, or taking on responsibility. (See Isaiah 9:6.)

Welcome

Welcome is a New Testament word, having been used only twice in Hebrew Scripture. Jesus was a welcoming person. Speaking to the Romans, Paul put Christ's welcoming nature into perspective: "Welcome one another, therefore, just as Christ has welcomed you, for the glory of God" (Romans 15:7).

Having traveled from town to town in his ministry, Jesus knows the importance of feeling welcome. The crowds welcomed Jesus as did Mary and the Galileans. (See Luke 8:40, 9:11, and 10:38; and John 4:45.) When you feel welcome, he told the seventy who were to go before him, "Whenever you enter a town and its people welcome you, eat what is set before you; cure the sick who are there, and say to them, 'The kingdom of God has come near to you' " (Luke 10:8-9).

Jesus also knows how it feels to be unwelcome. He instructed his disciples and the seventy appointed later what to do when they were not welcome. "But whenever you enter a town and they do not welcome you, go out into its streets and say, 'Even the dust of your town that clings to our feet, we wipe off in protest against you. Yet know this: the kingdom of God has come near' " (Luke 10:10-11). See earlier, Luke 9:5.

Jesus does not discriminate in his welcoming. He welcomes all to the table, the sinner, the undesirable, the person with disability, everyone. He would view our actions toward every other person and particularly toward those who are disadvantaged or in trouble as reflecting how we would treat him. "[A]nd [Jesus] said to them, 'Whoever welcomes this child in my name welcomes me, and whoever welcomes me welcomes the one who sent me; for the least among all of you is the greatest' " (Luke 9:48). See also Matthew 10:40, 18:5; and Mark 9:37.

Feeling welcomed has a transforming effect. Suddenly one counts. Suddenly one gains or regains possibility. The tax collector named Zacchaeus, receiving the affirming welcome of Jesus, in turn "hurried down and was happy to welcome him" into his home. (See Luke 19:5-7.)

Negatively put, "I was a stranger and you did not welcome me, naked and you did not give me clothing, sick and in prison and you did not visit me" (Matthew 25:43). In positive words, "... for I was hungry and you gave me food, I was thirsty and you gave me something to drink, I was a stranger and you welcomed me ... And when was it that we saw you a stranger and welcomed you...?" (Matthew 25:35-39).

4. Parallel Scriptures

Tax Collectors And Sinners

The writers of the Synoptic Gospels wanted readers to know that Jesus associated with more than a few tax collectors and sinners. Luke refers to "*all* the tax collectors and sinners" (Luke 15:1), while Mark says, "*many* tax collectors and sinners" (Mark 2:15). Again, Luke says, "a *large* crowd of tax collectors and others" (Luke 5:29).

Heralding life in the realm of God, Jesus comments about numerous others who follow because they have faith, as well as those who do not believe: "Jesus said to those who followed him, 'Truly I tell you, in no one in Israel have I found such faith. I tell you, *many* will come from east and west and will eat with Abraham and Isaac and Jacob in the kingdom of heaven' " (Matthew 8:10-11).

In the present parable the Pharisees and scribes say, presumably to one another, "This fellow welcomes sinners and eats with them" (Luke 15:2). At Levi's house, the Pharisees pose a question to the disciples, "Why does he eat with tax collectors and sinners?" (Mark 2:16b).

Lost Sheep Parable

Luke's version is about twenty words longer than that of Matthew and is more personal. Immediately involving the reader, Luke begins, " 'Which one of you, having ...' " (Luke 15:4). Matthew keeps the reader at a distance. He begins, " 'What do you think? If a shepherd has ...' " (Matthew 18:12).

Luke presupposes that the shepherd will find the lost sheep, saying, " 'When he has found ...' " (Luke 15:5). Matthew follows on his "If a shepherd" with "And if he finds it" (Matthew 18:13).

Luke places the search in the wilderness (Luke 15:4). For Matthew, it is "on the mountains" (Matthew 18:12). Luke uses "lost" throughout the parable while Matthew chooses "gone" or went "astray" until verse 14. Luke says, "go after" (Luke 15:4) and Matthew says "go in search of" (Matthew 18:12). Luke emphasizes the shepherd's persistence with "until he finds it" (Luke 15:4), while the less optimistic Matthew says, "And if he finds it" (Matthew 18:13). Only Luke shows the shepherd's additional act of compassion, "he lays it on his shoulders and rejoices" (Luke 15:5).

Both writers agree that there will be rejoicing; however, only Luke reports that the shepherd "calls together his friends and neighbors" to help him celebrate (Luke 15:6).

Luke uses the "Just so," which he couplets in the parable of The Lost Coin, to speak of the rejoicing in heaven. (See Luke 15:7.) Matthew says, "So" (Matthew 18:14). Luke says, "Just so, I tell you," where Matthew says, "truly I tell you" (Matthew 18:14).

Luke states the conclusion in positive terms, "there will be" (Luke 15:7). Whereas Matthew uses the negative "it is not the will ... that" (Matthew 18:14). With Luke's exuberance, the shepherd, the friends and neighbors, and "in heaven" all find joy. Matthew speaks only of the shepherd's rejoicing. Luke makes the connection with sinners who repent. Matthew says only, "one of these little ones" (Matthew 18:14).

5. Chat Room

Retiree: I thought churches were to be caring places. What is more precious to God than God's creation? Look at the shepherd who considered each sheep in the flock enough of a treasure to leave the others in search of that sheep.

Church Member: Churches are like anything else. It is easier, more fun, more efficient to spend time and effort and certainly budgeted money on what will benefit the whole rather than just one person who needs something.

Retiree: That's just the point. A church consists of people one by one. A church is a place of relationship. As we parishioners age and are less able, we feel phased out.

Church Member: Is not that as it should be? You have had your turn at leadership. You have put in your time. Let yourself rest now. Give the younger ones a chance.

Retiree: Churches are not we-they places, the younger and the older. We are people, people in relationship. We in our later years have not lived all these years for ignorance. We are still human treasures, a wealth of quiet perspective here to be tapped. We still count. As our spiritual and physical needs change, part of the work of the church is watchful awareness and anticipation of those changes. We are letting go of our former identities, to be sure, but we also are still discovering ourselves. We are still learning to listen to God's plan for us. God is still finding us.

Single Dad: Now considering lost coins, both symbolically and literally, I would speak for the single, working parent and for dual-working parents. I'm stuck in a different sort of wilderness. About

167

the best that I can do for my spiritual life is to breath a quick prayer as I drive by my church on the rush to work, but it is still *my* church.

The parceling out of my time is in a constant state of triage. Finding time is not a matter of turning on a light. There is no spare time for the finding. It's all spent time, spent mostly with worn-out energy.

Church Member: I don't think so. Finding time is like finding enough money. Beyond the extremes of poverty, finding time for what is important is a matter of prioritizing. Nourishing the spirit energizes us for keeping it all in perspective no matter how many directions we go in.

Single Dad: You really don't understand how difficult prioritizing is when making a living, doing the laundry, going to my daughter's volleyball game, and more all have to be done. I don't grouch about it, but I'm too fragmented all the time. Why don't you follow me around for 24 hours? But rest up first and don't plan to sit down for meals. They are all on the run.

Church Member: I really do understand some of it, at least. I juggled different things in different circumstances, but I juggled, too. How can we be the church to you?

Single Dad: I don't know. Part of me doesn't even think about it any more. Part of me misses church and yearns for what once was.

Church: I, the church, am a lost sheep.

Single Dad: Be patient. Hold on. We will find you.

Church: I, the church, am willing to be found. Turn on your light so you can see what you need to be looking for.

Church Member: We have had the lights on dim for too long. We are looking in worn-out places.

Single Dad: There are new places.

Church: Look for me with the intensity of a shepherd searching for a lost sheep. Look for me as that woman looked for the lost coin needed to pay the rent. Search for me and you will find me, the still life-giving church, waiting for your imagination, your sensitivity, your perceptivity, and your open, listening hearts.

Retiree: I will rejoice when we have found you.

Church Member: There will be rejoicing indeed. It will be a new, meaningful life for the church.

Single Dad: It may surprise you, Church, to hear this from me, but you still count. You are still a living treasure, and I still want to be found.

Parable 14

The Clever Crook

Luke 16:1-13

---

1. Text

Then Jesus said to the disciples, "There was a rich man who had a manager, and charges were brought to him that this man was squandering his property. [2] So he summoned him and said to him, 'What is this that I hear about you? Give me an accounting of your management, because you cannot be my manager any longer.' [3] Then the manager said to himself, 'What will I do, now that my master is taking the position away from me? I am not strong enough to dig, and I am ashamed to beg. [4] I have decided what to do so that, when I am dismissed as manager, people may welcome me into their homes.' [5] So, summoning his master's debtors one by one, he asked the first, 'How much do you owe my master?' [6] He answered, 'A hundred jugs of olive oil.' He said to him, 'Take your bill, sit down quickly, and make it fifty.' [7] Then he asked another, 'And how much do you owe?' He replied, 'A hundred containers of wheat.' He said to him, 'Take your bill and make it eighty.' [8] And his master commended the dishonest manager because he had acted shrewdly; for the children of this age are more shrewd in dealing with their own generation than are the children of light. [9] And I tell you, make friends for yourselves by means of dishonest wealth so that when it is gone, they may welcome you into the eternal homes.

171

[10] *"Whoever is faithful in a very little is faithful*
also in much; and whoever is dishonest in a very little
is dishonest also in much. [11] If then you have not
been faithful with the dishonest wealth, who will en-
trust to you the true riches? [12] And if you have not
been faithful with what belongs to another, who will
give you what is your own? [13] No slave can serve
two masters; for a slave will either hate the one and
love the other, or be devoted to the one and despise the
other. You cannot serve God and wealth."

2. What's Happening?

First Point Of Action

Jesus tells this story to his disciples. A rich man learns that his manager has been charged with squandering the man's property.

Second Point Of Action

The rich man calls the manager to him. He asks, "What is this I have heard about you?" Apparently he does not give him a chance to answer but tells him to give him an accounting of his work. He is going to fire him.

Third Point Of Action

The manager then wonders to himself what he will do now. He is not strong enough to dig and is too proud to beg. He decides to do something that, after he is dismissed, will cause people to welcome him into their homes.

Fourth Point Of Action

One by one, he summons the rich man's creditors.

Fifth Point Of Action

He tells the first of the creditors to sit down quickly and reduce his bill from 100 jugs of olive oil to fifty jugs.

Sixth Point Of Action

He tells the second to reduce his bill from 100 to eighty containers of wheat.

Seventh Point Of Action

His master commends the dishonest manager because he has acted shrewdly.

Eighth Point Of Action

He says the children of this age are more shrewd in dealing with their own generations than are the children of light. He says to make friends by means of dishonest wealth so that when it is gone, they may welcome you into the eternal homes (note homes).

Ninth Point Of Action

Jesus explains that whoever is faithful in a very little is faithful also in much, and whoever is dishonest in a very little is dishonest also in much.

Tenth Point Of Action

He asks two questions: Who will entrust you with the true riches if you have not been faithful with the dishonest wealth? Who will give you what is your own if you have not been faithful to another?

Eleventh Point Of Action

He concludes: No slave can serve two masters; for a slave will either hate the one and love the other, or be devoted to the one and despise the other. You cannot serve God and wealth.

3. Spadework

Dishonest

In addition to references to dishonesty in the present text are the few passages below. However sparse, they suggest that dishonesty is despicable. Moses' father-in-law advises him to get assistance with his work. "You should also look for able men among the people, men who fear God, are trustworthy, and hate dishonest gain" (Exodus 18:21).

Dishonesty is destructive: "Woe to him who builds his house by unrighteousness, and his upper rooms by injustice; who makes his neighbors work for nothing, and does not give them their wages" (Jeremiah 22:13). Jeremiah continues, "But your eyes and heart are only on your dishonest gain, for shedding innocent blood, and for practicing oppression and violence" (Jeremiah 22:17).

The prophet Ezekiel also lambasts dishonesty: See Ezekiel 22:13, 22:23-24, and 22:27: "Its officials within it are like wolves tearing the prey, shedding blood, destroying lives to get dishonest gain." Neither can the prophet Micah condone deceitful behavior: "Can I tolerate wicked scales and a bag of dishonest weights? Your wealthy are full of violence; your inhabitants speak lies, with tongues of deceit in their mouths. Therefore I have begun to strike you down, making you desolate because of your sins" (Micah 6:11-13).

Eternal Home(s)

The present passage alone says, "eternal homes": "And I tell you, make friends for yourselves by means of dishonest wealth so that when it is gone, they may welcome you into the eternal *homes*" (Luke 16:9). Is "homes" subtle mention of the two possible directions after physical life? Ecclesiastes uses this death metaphor in the singular: When life changes and "when one is afraid of heights, and terrors are in the road; the almond tree blossoms, the grasshopper drags itself along and desire fails; because all must go to their eternal home" (Ecclesiastes 12:5). See also Psalm 49:14 and 2 Corinthians 5:8-10.

Faithful

Are we faithful because God is faithful to us? "For your steadfast love is before my eyes, / and I walk in faithfulness to you" (Psalm 26:3).

Is that what keeps us going during the rough times? "For the Lord is good; / his steadfast love endures forever, / and his faithfulness to all generations" (Psalm 100:5) and "Steadfast love and faithfulness will meet; / righteousness and peace will kiss each other. / Faithfulness will spring up from the ground, / and righteousness will look down from the sky" (Psalm 85:10-11).

Is being faithful to what is in our heart and mind enough? "Know therefore that the Lord your God is God, the faithful God who maintains covenant loyalty with those who love him and keep his commandments, to a thousand generations" (Deuteronomy 7:9).

Can we pattern our faithfulness after the faithfulness of God? God is "without deceit, just and upright is he." (See Deuteronomy 32:4.) "The works of his hands are faithful and just; / all his precepts are trustworthy" (Psalm 111:7). God is "faithful in all his words, / and gracious in all his deeds" (Psalm 145:13).

In response to our faithfulness, does God look with special favor upon those who "turn to [God] in their hearts" (Psalm 85:8)? "But know that the Lord has set apart the faithful for himself; / the Lord hears when I call to him" (Psalm 4:3). Despite what appears to be an ever-increasing need to buy more necessary things, great monetary gain need not be the indicator of a successful and meaningful existence. (See also Psalm 97:10.)

Which is the greater sacrifice — love of God or money? "Gather to me my faithful ones, / who made a covenant with me by sacrifice!" (Psalm 50:5).

Why not trust in God's providence? "Into your hand I commit my spirit; / you have redeemed me, O Lord, faithful God" (Psalm 31:5). See also Psalm 31:23 and 37:28.

Dare we hope? "Let us hold fast to the confession of our hope without wavering, for he who has promised is faithful" (Hebrews 10:23). "No testing has overtaken you that is not common to everyone. God is faithful, and he will not let you be tested beyond your strength, but with the testing he will also provide the way out so that you may be able to endure it" (1 Corinthians 10:13). "But as for me, my prayer is to you, O Lord. / At an acceptable time, O God, / in the abundance of your steadfast love, answer me. / With your faithful help rescue me from sinking in the mire; / let me be delivered from my enemies / and from the deep waters" (Psalm 69:13-14). See also Psalm 30:4 and 32:6. (Twenty-seven of the 91 references to "faithful" appear in Psalms, as well as 35 of the 68 references to "faithfulness.")

Faithful is also doing what is good and right before God. (See 2 Chronicles 31:20.) Faithful is "faithful deeds in accordance with what is written in the law of the Lord" (2 Chronicles 35:26). The faithful person respects God. (See Nehemiah 7:2.) Faithful is found in the heart. (See Nehemiah 9:8.)

Manager

Two references to "manager" in addition to the present text include, first, the manager of the vineyard, whose equal pay for unequal work hours parallels the love of God for all people regardless of their condition. (See Matthew 20:8.) The second reference speaks of the "faithful and prudent manager" the master trusted to oversee his slaves. (See Luke 12:42.)

The writer of 1 Timothy speaks of the prerequisite of managing one's household well before taking care of God's church. See 1 Timothy 3:4-5 and 3:12. See also 1 Timothy 5:14.

Master

How to serve a master: Show steadfast love (Genesis 24:14c); do not forsake steadfast love and faithfulness (Genesis 24:27); deal loyally and truly with the master (Genesis 24:49); acknowledge God's role in your life — "His master saw that the Lord was with him, and that the Lord caused all that he did to prosper in his hands" (Genesis 39:3).

"Remember the word that I said to you, 'Servants are not greater than their master.' If they persecuted me, they will persecute you; if they kept my word, they will keep yours also" (John 15:20).

Paul admonished the Colossian slave masters to treat their slaves "justly and fairly, for you know that you also have a Master in heaven." (See Colossians 4:1.)

Serve God

In addition to the versions of the present text in Matthew and Luke, "serve God" appears in two other references, both from the prophet Malachi: "You have said, 'It is vain to serve God. What do we profit by keeping his command or by going about as mourners before the Lord of hosts?' " (Malachi 3:14) and "Then once more you shall see the difference between the righteous and the wicked, between one who serves God and one who does not serve him" (Malachi 3:18).

176

Squander

To squander is to waste, to spend foolishly, engage in too many splurges, to throw away through too many extravagant expenditures. Both the younger prodigal son (Luke 15:13ff, Parable 4, Cycle C) and the dishonest manager in the present parable get into trouble because of squandering.

Trustworthy

"The works of his hands are faithful and just; all his precepts are trustworthy" (Psalm 111:7). "His master said to him, 'Well done, good and trustworthy slave; you have been trustworthy in a few things, I will put you in charge of many things; enter into the joy of your master' " (Matthew 25:21 and Luke 19:17). See also Exodus 18:21 above.

Unfaithful

"What if some were unfaithful? Will their faithlessness nullify the faithfulness of God? By no means! Although everyone is a liar, let God be proved true, as it is written, 'So that you may be justified in your words, and prevail in your judging' " (Romans 3:3-4).

What about the unfaithful? "The faithful will abound with blessings, but one who is in a hurry to be rich will not go unpunished" (Proverbs 28:20). "He will guard the feet of his faithful ones, but the wicked shall be cut off in darkness; for not by might does one prevail" (1 Samuel 2:9). "A faithful witness does not lie, / but a false witness breathes out lies" (Proverbs 14:5).

Not only today do we wonder where the people of good character have gone: "Help, O Lord, for there is no longer anyone who is godly; / the faithful have disappeared from humankind" (Psalm 12:1). And how would these words apply today in Israel? "I am one of those who are peaceable and faithful in Israel; you seek to destroy a city that is a mother in Israel; why will you swallow up the heritage of the Lord?" (2 Samuel 20:19).

Wealth

Pay attention to the role of God in your wealth: "Do not say to yourself, 'My power and the might of my own hand have gotten me this wealth.' But remember the Lord your God, for it is he who gives you power to get wealth, so that he may confirm his covenant that he swore to your ancestors, as he is doing today" (Deuteronomy 8:17-18).

God also bestowed upon Solomon all that he had not asked for — "possessions, wealth, honor, or the life of those who hate you, and have not even asked for long life" in addition to the wisdom and knowledge that he had asked for to be a good king. (See 2 Chronicles 1:11.) "I walk in the way of righteousness, / along the paths of justice, / endowing with wealth those who love me, / and filling their treasuries" (Proverbs 8:20-21). "Likewise all to whom God gives wealth and possessions and whom he enables to enjoy them, and to accept their lot and find enjoyment in their toil — this is the gift of God" (Ecclesiastes 5:19).

Wealth and the lack of it carry other surprises: "Wealth hastily gotten will dwindle, but those who gather little by little will increase it" (Proverbs 13:11); "Some pretend to be rich, yet have nothing; others pretend to be poor, yet have great wealth. Wealth is a ransom for a person's life, but the poor get no threats" (Proverbs 13:7-8); and "Like the partridge hatching what it did not lay, so are all who amass wealth unjustly; in mid-life it will leave them, and at their end they will prove to be fools" (Jeremiah 17:11).

Trust in the wrong things can have disastrous results: "The righteous will see, and fear, / and will laugh at the evildoer, saying, / 'See the one who would not take / refuge in God, / but trusted in abundant riches, / and sought refuge in wealth!' " (Psalm 52:6-7). See also Psalm 49:5-9.

Christ expressed clearly his view about wealth: "Then Jesus looked around and said to his disciples, 'How hard it will be for those who have wealth to enter the kingdom of God!' " (Mark 10:23), and "As for what was sown among thorns, this is the one who hears the word, but the cares of the world and the lure of wealth choke the word, and it yields nothing" (Matthew 13:22). See also Mark 4:19.

4. Parallel Scripture

Matthew 6:24 and Luke 16:13 are identical presentations of the "no one can serve two masters passage" except that Matthew's begins "No one" whereas Luke's starts as "No slave."

5. Chat Room

Donald Waller: Everybody does it. Look at business. How are you going to make a profit without mark-ups? Agreed, above the standard mark-up, there is a line. It depends upon what the public will tolerate. A certain category of people will expect a huge mark-up. They enjoy the boasting prestige about the price they paid.

Pat Boccardi: That is a relatively small group compared to the rest of us who budget and spend with prudence.

Waller: You have to remember that I need to get paid for my efforts. I need to live, too. I have a family to support, things to do. I should get some benefit. I expend considerable managerial energy. I earn my bonuses.

Boccardi: Bonuses usually are not self-assigned. Fair is fair, but inflated value is a balloon and ultimately damaging. Customers are not stupid.

Waller: It's a game. Customers do not need to know everything. Besides, what is one customer when you survey the whole picture? What does a little skimming here and a little overlooking there matter? I play all the angles. Is that not the job of a good manager?

Boccardi: A good manager is an honest manager. A little scheming here and a little overleaping there adds up to a pretty sour conscience.

Waller: I dismissed conscience a long time ago. Why should I listen to my conscience when my gut feeling says, "Make a killing on these vulnerable people now"?

179

Boccardi: Janice Taylor, are you online?

Janice Taylor: I'm on.

Boccardi: How did things get so out of hand that you had to let go of your manager?

Taylor: That's what happens when you trust. Now do not misunderstand. They must play the games of today to remain competitive. I want my manager to be sharp and to have a good sense of the practical.

Boccardi: To be shrewd, even cunning?

Taylor: Of course, when necessary. When you oversee an operation, you need sound judgment and, at times, special resourcefulness. But I personally do not want to be bruised.

Boccardi: As long as you come out ahead?

Taylor: Making the projected level of money involves compromise.

John Demitz: I have some thoughts about this. At first, when Mr. Waller reduced my debt, I felt pretty good, relieved actually. The more I thought about it, I think the whole business over there is crooked.

Boccardi: That matters to you even though you gained some benefit?

Demitz: Actually, I have been repaying the relieved debt, the balance that I would have owed them. I cannot do something at another person's expense and that is what it would have led to.

Boccardi: That is virtuous.

Demitz: Money has always been tight for me. Sometimes I get behind, but somehow I have always found a way to skimp and get by. We haven't starved yet. I just have to keep everything in perspective — my family, what is right between God and me, my priorities.

Boccardi: Then you have a higher rule.

Demitz: What it is, is that I have to be able to live with myself. I must be faithful to my values. Were I to buy into their system, I would feel compromised. Mr. Waller would expect things from me that I could not in my heart do for him.

Boccardi: You do not want to be part of the game, even at a loss to you.

Demitz: It depends upon what you mean by loss. No, I cannot be part of their game. I cannot serve two masters. Dare I risk economic survival with honesty? It has been done. There are basically honest people around in all businesses and professions. In my heart, I have chosen the way of faithfulness.

Parable 15

Rich Man, Poor Man

Luke 16:19-31

---

1. Text

"There was a rich man who was dressed in pure and fine linen and who feasted sumptuously every day. [20] And at his gate lay a poor man named Lazarus, covered with sores, [21] who longed to satisfy his hunger with what fell from the rich man's table; even the dogs would come and lick his sores. [22] The poor man died and was carried away by the angels to be with Abraham. The rich man also died and was buried. [23] In Hades, where he was being tormented, he looked up and saw Abraham far away with Lazarus by his side. [24] He called out, 'Father Abraham, have mercy on me, and send Lazarus to dip the tip of his finger in water and cool my tongue; for I am in agony in these flames.' [25] But Abraham said, 'Child, remember that during your lifetime you received your good things, and Lazarus in like manner evil things; but now he is comforted here, and you are in agony. [26] Besides all this, between you and us a great chasm has been fixed, so that those who might want to pass from here to you cannot do so, and no one can cross from there to us.' [27] He said, 'Then, father, I beg you to send him to my father's house — [28] for I have five brothers — that he may warn them, so that they will not also come into this place of torment.' [29] Abraham replied, 'They have Moses and the prophets; they should listen to them.' [30] He said, 'No, father Abraham; but if someone goes to them from the

*dead, they will repent.' [31] He said to him, 'If they do
not listen to Moses and the prophets, neither will they
be convinced even if someone rises from the dead.' "*

2. What's Happening?

First Point Of Action

Jesus presents the lifetime situations of the rich man's opulence and Lazarus' poverty.

Second Point of Action

Jesus presents the afterlife conditions of the agony of the rich man and the comfort of Lazarus.

Third Point of Action

The rich man and Father Abraham talk: Abraham's expression of justice; Abraham's "Besides"; the rich man's understanding of his situation; the rich man's request for his five brothers; and Abraham's lost cause conclusion.

3. Spadework

Crossing The Chasm

Of the sixty references in Hebrew Scripture that use Sheol, fifteen contain the phrase, "down to Sheol." (See Genesis 37:35.) The terms "heaven" and "Sheol" reflect the ancient belief in a three-story universe: "If I ascend to heaven, you are there; if I make my bed in Sheol, you are there" (Psalm 139:8) and "Can you find out the deep things of God? Can you find out the limit of the Almighty? It is higher than heaven — what can you do? Deeper than Sheol — what can you know?" (Job 11:7-8).

Present-day folk could choose to dismiss hell and heaven talk because we know about the multiplicity of universes within the galaxy, the geological formation of the earth, and own other sophisticated scientific knowledge. We could choose to see through the eyes of a metaphor that wants to describe some other place besides the present, known world. If a heaven exists, as a realm of yearned-for hope that draws us forward, then a hell also exists, as a realm of unmitigated chaos, the thought of which prods us toward a higher standard of living on earth.

"Father Abraham" suggests that these three realms are separated by chasms as wide as a piece of Lexan is impermeable. The helping hand is helpless here. "[T]hose who might want to pass from here to you cannot do so, and no one can cross from there to us" (Luke 16:26).

Hades

Before the time of Christ, Hades was the underworld of classical Greek and Roman mythology, the place beneath the earth where the souls of the dead go. Is Sheol inevitable? "Who can live and never see death? / Who can escape the power of Sheol?" (Psalm 89:48). These words sound benign and neutral, as if everyone who dies automatically visits Sheol first. Yet these same words also hint of learned or perhaps intuitive overtones of penalty.

The world-spanning collection of explanatory myths and stories that most members of the human family espouse addresses these questions that all people ponder: What happens after we die? Is no one "good enough" to go straight to "heaven"? Will we actually have to pay for our sins? What happened to atonement and forgiveness through Christ? Will the varieties of hell we experience during our lifetime continue after death? Do they count for anything later on? Is there any mercy? What about justice? Is God really in charge of our lives? Myth, folklore, legend, and tradition merge with the stories of our faith to offer answers.

The realm of Sheol (Hebrew term) and its New Testament-exclusive counterpart, Hades or hell, holds a further connotation. Sheol is in the realm of its being too late for a person. Sheol is translated "the grave" in the King James Version. Hell appears in the New Testament a dozen times. Once, in Matthew 5:22, hell is translated as "the judgment" (KJV). In the remaining New Testament references, the KJV uses hell for the New Revised Standard Version, Hades. One instance of Hades in the Gospels is from today's parable: "In Hades, where he was being tormented, he looked up and saw Abraham far away with Lazarus by his side" (Luke 16:23).

"Wilderness" occurs 239 times in the Bible. "Desert" appears 54 times in the Old and New Testaments. Contrasted to Hades, wilderness and desert are definite, geographical places that might also be arenas of physical exile, hardship, temptation, and struggle. In a wilderness, a person might die from lack of material things like water and food or from isolation. Wilderness also can be a metaphorical, "state of being" place of wandering and working out the problems of one's life. Sheol adds the times that a physical or mental disability becomes handicapping, such as coming upon a flight of steps that closes the door to one who is wheelchair-mobile. Sheol adds economic impoverishment, chaotic relationships, and the refusal of insurance for those with chronic illnesses.

Wilderness, desert, the Pit, Sheol, Hades, and hell are uncomfortable words that percolate throughout the Bible. First mention of "the pit" is that into which Joseph was thrown by his brothers. (See Genesis 37.) For the Hebrews, perhaps all reference to the pit held the shadow of that first pit. Job, the Psalms, and the books of the Prophets are filled with sixty of the seventy Old and New Testament references to "the pit" or "the Pit." (See Job 33:18-30; Psalm 16:10, 29:1, and 30:9.)

For the writer of Revelation, "the pit" becomes "the bottomless pit." "They have as king over them the angel of the bottomless pit; his name in Hebrew is Abaddon [that is, Destruction], and in Greek he is called Apollyon [that is Destroyer]" (Revelation 9:11). See also Revelation 9:1-2, 11:7, 17:8, and 20:1. "Sheol is naked before God, and Abaddon has no covering" (Job 26:6). The name, Abaddon, is found five other times in the Bible. (See Job 28:22 and 31:12; Psalm 88:11; and Proverbs 15:11 and 27:20.) Of the 41 biblical references to Satan, 33 appear in the New Testament. Devil, used 49 times, is New Testament specific.

The worst option of Hades appears to be if one were sent alive to Sheol: "But if the Lord creates something new, and the ground opens its mouth and swallows them up, with all that belongs to them, and they go down alive into Sheol, then you shall know that these men have despised the Lord" (Numbers 16:30). See also Psalm 55:15.

Mercy

Does God punish forever with the worst images of torture that one can conjure? Descriptions of hell are desperate: "[T]he cords of Sheol entangled me, the snares of death confronted me" (2 Samuel 22:6 and Psalm 18:5). However, even Sheol is not a hopeless state of being: " 'I called to the Lord out of my distress, and he answered me; out of the belly of Sheol I cried, and you heard my voice' " (Jonah 2:2).

Sheol is not a place or state of permanent residence. God rescues or brings one out of Sheol: "The Lord kills and brings to life; he brings down to Sheol and raises up" (1 Samuel 2:6). God does not abandon an individual in Sheol. God hears cries from Sheol and responds by restoring the soul: "O Lord my God, I cried to you for help, and you have healed me. O Lord, you brought up my soul from Sheol, restored me to life from among those gone down to the Pit" (Psalm 30:2-3).

The love of God wins over our human need for retribution: "For great is your steadfast love toward me; you have delivered my soul from the depths of Sheol" (Psalm 86:13). The mystery of God suggests that God is in charge of it all: "The Lord kills and brings to life; he brings down to Sheol and raises up" (1 Samuel 2:6).

Parable

The heart of a parable lies in what the story suggests to us, with what we connect at a level beyond its words, within the silence between the parable and where the parable meets us and we meet its truth.

The Vulnerable Person, Lazarus

In this parable, Lazarus has no voice. Christ gives him being by naming him. Consider what part of each of us is a Lazarus — the vulnerability, the being seen as invisible, the object of injustice, the scapegoat for our own feelings of threat, the part of our identity that is beyond our control. Consider who in the community, family, and work place or school are named Lazarus.

The Rich Man

The rich man is excessively rich, wearing purple and the latest fashion of finest linen. He eats at four star restaurants, jets anywhere at will, owns a home here and a house there, lobbies government, and pays off others without a twinge of conscience. He is highly influential, ambulates with a definite swagger, does not mind crunching people in his way, and Christ does not give him a name.

The rich man uses everyone, even calling upon Lazarus to be his servant in Hades. Remember, the Pharisees were lovers of money. (See Luke 16:14.) Christ did not dignify those who ridiculed him with a name.

4. Parallel Scripture

Status Of Lazarus

Lazarus "longed to satisfy his hunger with what fell from the rich man's table; even the dogs would come and lick his sores" (Luke 16:21). The Canaanite woman said, "Yes, Lord, yet even the dogs eat the crumbs that fall from their masters' table" (Matthew 15:27). Christ's response toward the most vulnerable was compassion. The impoverished are not far from God's presence. "Take care that you do not despise one of these little ones; for, I tell you, in heaven their angels continually see the face of my Father in heaven" (Matthew 18:10).

Equity, Parity, And Retribution

Abraham told the rich man he had received his good things during his lifetime. Lazarus had received his share of evil things during his lifetime. Now, the rich man will know agony and Lazarus will find comfort. Revelation 20:13 speaks of all being judged "according to what they had done." Again, Jesus lambasts the religious leaders of his day in the Lukan Beatitudes and Woes: "But woe to you who are rich, for you have received your consolation" (Luke 6:24). See Luke 6:20-24 and Matthew 5:1-12. "Do not fear those who kill the body but cannot kill the soul; rather fear him who can destroy both soul and body in hell" (Matthew 10:28).

Religious Heritage

Earlier in Luke, the writer reminds us to concentrate on how we live rather than to count on our connection with the church and its foreparents to run interference for us on judgment day: "Bear fruits worthy of repentance. Do not begin to say to yourselves, 'We have Abraham as our ancestor'; for I tell you, God is able from these stones to raise up children to Abraham" (Luke 3:8). On the other hand, the God-connection does count. Jesus said to the chief tax collector, Zacchaeus, "Today salvation has come to this house, because he too is a son of Abraham" (Luke 19:9).

The final word returns us to ourselves. We must remember whose we are as children of God rather than rely on the ostensible and ostentatious, yet empty practice of religion: "Do not think that I will accuse you before the Father; your accuser is Moses, on whom you have set your hope. If you believed Moses, you would believe me, for he wrote about me. But if you do not believe what he wrote, how will you believe what I say?" (John 5:45-47).

5. Chat Room

Office Worker: My mother used to threaten my errant sister with sending her out to the bogey man she said lived in the shed at the rear of our property. Just the thought of that bogey man was enough to rearrange my behavior.

Supervisor: Somebody has to be faulted for the wrongs of an individual. It is hard to accept blame. Blame Nemesis, the Greek goddess of punishment and revenge. Blame the Egyptian goddess of evil and the underworld, Taourt. Blame the "tro wo," minor Ashanti folk gods who toy with the Ghanian people. Blame Chernobog, the Slavic god of disorder and hell. Blame Azazel, Leviticus demon of the wilderness. (See Leviticus 16:8-10.)

Office Worker: Are you into all that? I'm impressed.

Supervisor: I dabble. What I am saying, though, is that we feel somebody has to be in charge so we can find order in the turmoil or maybe so we designate a scapegoat.

Office Worker: It is safer to have a Hades, a Sheol, or a hell down there somewhere in some place than to admit that the chaos is as close as within our own soul.

Supervisor: That's right. Somebody has to bring retribution. Anything but taking responsibility for ourselves.

Para-legal: I have a comment. I'm over on corridor three. I keep hearing the rich man's call to Father Abraham. To whom do you cry out when you are in trouble? Does the child within you cry out to Mama, Daddy? Do you cry out to a spouse? To Jesus? To God? Who is your Father Abraham? Does your cry for help just break into empty air?

Supervisor: The cry of the rich one does haunt me. He could not have been all that bad. When he found out it was too late for him, he did think about someone else. It sounds to me as if this is one of those you-reap-what-you-sow stories.

Para-legal: Could be. Say, this chat room knows no temporal or geographical boundaries. Why not attempt to get those two online? Wait a minute. They are already chat listed. Let's follow their conversation.

Rich Person: Father Abraham said no one can cross the chasm.

Lazarus: I am acquainted with hell. There are bridges.

Rich Person: Think about the great chasm between you and me — my superb health, the quantity of my tangible possessions, the capacity to do pretty much as I please. I fail to see how any of these things have earned me a home in hell. What is wrong with opulence? Why should I not make the most of what I have? Why not flaunt my inheritance? I earned my purple robe.

Lazarus: How you received or how you used your wealth might be the trouble. The issue may be the emptiness within your soul, the false friends, the chasm of your unwillingness to understand others, your ignoring folk like me as if we were stones. It could be the chasm of faulty relationships with those less fortunate than you or even with those equal to you. It could be the chasm of lack of understanding in situations of injustice.

Rich Person: You need not go on and on. Why are you so much better than I am that you get to go to heaven?

Lazarus: I'm not "better than." This is not a game of one-upmanship. I have known a lifetime of physical pain and inability. My constant lack of enough money has robbed me of any parity or chance of recompense for my present condition. These things alone do not make me better or worse than you. It has to do with what governs from within.

Para-legal: Greetings, all. I have been following your dialogue and wonder about this place called Hades. Do you not think that concept is a bit outdated? Even given the image of the molten core of the earth, we no longer believe in a three-story universe.

Supervisor: Outmoded or not, even in our era of ignoring authority figures, we seem to need some place, some external force to threaten us into better behavior. Even if we need to upgrade the images of its terror, the human community offers a variety of explanations for the inexplicable. But listen —

Rich Person: But, Lazarus, will I be stuck here forever?

Lazarus: Listen to these words: "But God will ransom my / soul from the power / of Sheol, / for he will receive me" (Psalm 49:15). And hear these words: "For great is your steadfast / love toward me; / you have delivered my soul / from the depths of Sheol" (Psalm 86:13).

I have spent a lifetime of gaining strength from these Psalms. I believed that my suffering could not, would not, go on and on. Neither will yours.

Rich Person: How do you know about all that? You are uneducated.

Lazarus: I am disadvantaged, not stupid. My ears and my heart are open. You would be surprised by what I gleaned there by your gate. These words are my favorite: "If I ascend to heaven, you / are there; / if I make my bed in Sheol, / you are there" (Psalm 139:8). So, you see, even you with all your selfishness and your veneer of arrogance are not sunk. As far as I can tell, God refuses to abandon either of us.

Rich Person: It troubled me greatly when Father Abraham said I had received my good things during my lifetime, so now after death, I get the agony. Sounds as if we are each apportioned an equal amount of good things and evil things. If that is so, then every person whose life is filled with good things has a real mess to look forward to later.

Lazarus: I hope that does not follow. I can only say that we all have those preconditions that set our course. A disease process, once begun, sets up a chain reaction of bodily or mental changes. Some can be turned around with appropriate care. Some cannot. So it is with chronic behavior. Some people can change their habits and others cannot.

Rich Person: Look how many years you lay at my gate. Was it laziness on your part? You could have done something to help yourself. Why should having a debilitating illness set you apart?

Lazarus: First, I may have appeared lazy to you. I was always there when people came by. They talked to me. Hell is a state of being wherein something has power over us. It is beyond our control. Hell is the chasm of human impossibility.

Rich Person: Father Abraham said it was too late for me. So what do you think about his telling me my five brothers are not savable? It took my getting down here to turn me around. I know my brothers. That is what they need, a representative from hell to enlighten

192

them. Would not my concern for them get Father Abraham on my side?

Lazarus: It is not a matter of whom he sends to teach your brothers, but rather if they would choose to become teachable. In any guise, false religion is faulty religion. Actually, I think taking responsibility for the way we live our lives is the point of our parable. We are each responsible for our choices and willingness to improve our ways. I must say, however, that your concern for someone beside yourself did sound like a positive change.

Rich Person: Might I ask then, Lazarus, from where does your hope come? You have been saddled with all these disabilities and illnesses all your life.

Lazarus: I know a merciful God. Part of mercy is patience, and patience brings endurance. I believe that hope lies somewhere in the midst of all that. When Father Abraham addressed you, he called you "Child." Child is spoken by someone who cares about you. No matter who you are or how your life has been, remember that you are still a child of God. Were I you, I would opt for hope as the end result of all the turmoil, even yours.

Parable 16

A Decent Obsession

Luke 17:5-10

---

1. Text

The apostles said to the Lord, "Increase our faith!"
[6] The Lord replied, "If you had faith the size of a
mustard seed, you could say to this mulberry tree, 'Be
uprooted and planted in the sea,' and it would obey you.

[7] "Who among you would say to your slave who
has just come in from plowing or tending sheep in the
field, 'Come here at once and take your place at the
table'? [8] Would you not rather say to him, 'Prepare
supper for me, put on your apron and serve me while I
eat and drink; later you may eat and drink'? [9] Do
you thank the slave for doing what was commanded?
[10] So you also, when you have done all that you were
ordered to do, say, 'We are worthless slaves; we have
done only what we ought to have done!'"

2. What's Happening?

First Point Of Action

The disciples ask Jesus to increase their faith.

Second Point Of Action

Jesus offers the metaphor of a tiny seed. If you had faith the size of a mustard seed and ordered a mulberry tree to be uprooted and planted in the sea, it would obey.

195

Third Point Of Action

Jesus asks who would invite your slave who had just come in from plowing or tending the sheep to come at once and take your place at the table. Would you not command that the slave prepare and serve your supper and then later the slave may eat and drink?

Fourth Point Of Action

Jesus asked a second question. Do you thank the slave for doing what was commanded?

Fifth Point Of Action

Jesus concluded that when we have done all that we were ordered, we also say that we are worthless slaves; we have done only what we ought to have done. This answers how we can increase our faith.

3. Spadework

Mustard Seed/Mulberry Tree

The mulberry is a strong tree, as shown in the other reference to the mulberry. "As a gift one chooses mulberry wood — wood that will not rot — then seeks out a skilled artisan to set up an image that will not topple" (Isaiah 40:20).

Ought

The "ought," the obligation or duty, the desirability, advisability, or prudence of an action, weighs heavily upon us. Of the 45 "ought" references, ten are from the four gospels, 21 from the epistles, and nine from Hebrew Scripture.

The "ought" advises in regard to wrongful sexual relations. (See Genesis 20:9 and 34:7.) The "ought" advises in regard to sinning by doing any of "the things that by commandments of the Lord his God ought not to be done and incurs guilt" (Leviticus 4:22). See also Leviticus 4:13, 4:27, and 5:17. Wise people and those who understand the times know what ought to be done. (See 1 Kings 2:9 and 1 Chronicles 12:32.)

The Holy Spirit teaches what ought to be said. (See Luke 12:12.) The familiar Romans 7:14-20 passage about our not doing what we want to do and doing the very thing we hate transposes to the "ought."

Servant

This Exodus passage suggests a distinction among "slave," "servant," and "bound or hired servant." "... but any slave who has been purchased may eat of it after he has been circumcised; no bound or hired servant may eat of it" (Exodus 12:44b-45).

Most of the 350 "servant" references come as "my servant Moses," "Moses, the servant of the Lord," "your servant Israel," "your servant David," "servant of," etc. Appearing 37 times in the Psalms, "servant" speaks of our relationship to God: "Deal with your servant according to your steadfast love, / and teach me your statutes. / I am your servant; give me understanding, / so that I may know your decrees" (Psalm 119:124-125).

"Servant" is an important concept for Isaiah. See especially the "Servant Songs" — Isaiah 42:1-4, 49:1-6, and 50:4-9. "Here is my servant, whom I uphold, my chosen, in whom my soul delights; I have put my spirit upon him; he will bring forth justice to the nations" (Isaiah 42:1).

The "servant" metaphor is also key in Jesus' life. Mary, the mother of Jesus, saw herself as a servant of God. See the Magnificat (Luke 1:46-48) and Luke 1:38. God affirms Jesus: "Here is my servant, whom I have chosen, my beloved, with whom my soul is well pleased. I will put my Spirit upon him, and he will proclaim justice to the Gentiles" (Matthew 12:18). Jesus defines relationship as servanthood: "The greatest among you will be your servant" (Matthew 23:11). Then there are the "first must be last" passages: "He sat down, called the twelve, and said to them, 'Whoever wants to be first must be last of all and servant of all'" (Mark 9:35). See also Matthew 19:30, 20:16, and 20:26-28; Mark 10:43-44; Luke 13:30; and John 13:12-18.

The writer of John upgrades the relationship from "servants" to "friends": "I do not call you servants any longer, because the servant does not know what the master is doing; but I have called you friends, because I have made known to you everything that I have heard from my Father" (John 15:15).

Serve

First mention of the 163 references to "serve" as a command to a slave servant was from Joseph. (See Genesis 43:31.) Serving strangers in a foreign land was seen both as the result of defeat in battle and punishment from God. "When the Lord has given you rest from your pain and turmoil and the hard service with which you were made to serve, you will take up this taunt against the king of Babylon" (Isaiah 14:3-4). "And when your people say, 'Why has the Lord our God done all these things to us?' you shall say to them, 'As you have forsaken me and served foreign gods in your land, so you shall serve strangers in a land that is not yours' " (Jeremiah 5:19). See also Jeremiah 15:14 and 17:4.

As a result of battle defeat or negotiation, anyone could become enslaved. "When you draw near to a town to fight against it, offer it terms of peace. If it accepts your terms of peace and surrenders to you, then all the people in it shall serve you at forced labor" (Deuteronomy 20:10-11). Remember the familiar challenge by Goliath: " 'If he is able to fight with me and kill me, then we will be your servants; but if I prevail against him and kill him, then you shall be our servants and serve us' " (1 Samuel 17:9). See also 1 Samuel 11:1.

Those who served kings were a different sort of person. (See Proverbs 22:29.) Hear King Rehoboam's advisors, a possible prelude to today's parable:

> And they sent and called him; and Jeroboam and all the assembly of Israel came and said to Rehoboam, "Your father made our yoke heavy. Now therefore lighten the hard service of your father and his heavy yoke that he placed on us, and we will serve you." He said to them, "Go away for three days, then come again to me." So the people went away.
> Then King Rehoboam took counsel with the older men who had attended his father Solomon while he was still alive, saying, "How do you advise me to answer

198

this people?" They answered him, "If you will be a ser-
vant to this people today and serve them, and speak
good words to them when you answer them, then they
will be your servants forever."   — 1 Kings 12:3-7

The parable of the Watching Servants also refers to serving one's servants: "Blessed are those slaves whom the master finds alert when he comes; truly I tell you, he will fasten his belt and have them sit down to eat, and he will come and serve them" (Luke 12:37). (See Luke 12:32-40, Parable 9, Cycle C.)

Here it is again, a prophet asking a servant how he can serve her. When creditors threatened to take her daughters into slavery, the wife of a deceased servant of Elisha reminded Elisha that her husband had been God-fearing, whereupon Elisha asked what he could do for her. The generous man instructed her to borrow empty vessels "and not just a few" from neighbors. (See 2 Kings 4:3ff.) See also 2 Kings 4:12ff.

Levite priests were called from age 25-40 to serve the people. (See Numbers 8:26.) The man from Bethlehem of Judah came to the house of Micah saying he would find a place anywhere he could to live. Micah invited him to stay with him and be like a father and a priest. (See Judges 17:11-18:4.)

The New Testament offers the benchmark of service to others:

But Jesus called them to him and said, "You know that
the rulers of the Gentiles lord it over them, and their
great ones are tyrants over them. It will not be so among
you; but whoever wishes to be great among you must
be your servant, and whoever wishes to be first among
you must be your slave; just as the Son of Man came
not to be served but to serve, and to give his life a ran-
som for many."   — Matthew 20:25-28
(See also Mark 10:41-45.)

In Jacob and Rachel's love story, the first seven years that Jacob voluntarily served Rachel's father "seemed to him but a few days because of the love he had for her" (Genesis 29:20). Because of his kinship with Laban, Laban would not allow him to serve for nothing and paid him a wage.

Serve Me [God]

Of the twelve references to "serve me" are those to "serve me as priests." (See Exodus 28:1, 28:4, 28:41, 29:1, 29:44, 40:30, and 40:15; Ezekiel 44:13; and Genesis 29:15.) Serving God requires following God. Serving is honorable: "Whoever serves me must follow me, and where I am, there will my servant be also. Whoever serves me, the Father will honor" (John 12:26). See also Malachi 3:18.

Service

Most of the 117 "service" references occur as household service or service in the tabernacle by the Levite priests.

Slave

Jesus uses the term "slave" as an apt metaphor: The ungrateful son in the Prodigal Sons Parable complained he had worked *like a slave* for his father without appropriate appreciation (Luke 15:29) and "Very truly, I tell you, everyone who commits sin is a slave to sin. The slave does not have a permanent place in the household; the son has a place there forever" (John 8:34b-35).

Slaves, bought from other Hebrews and taken as war booty, were referred to as "homeborn slave and the resident alien" (Exodus 23:12). For a man without a male heir, a slave might take on a special relationship: "And Abram said, 'You have given me no offspring, and so a slave born in my house is to be my heir'" (Genesis 15:3).

Sometimes, living in bondage was merciless. "The Egyptians became ruthless in imposing tasks on the Israelites, and made their lives bitter with hard service in mortar and brick and in every kind of field labor. They were ruthless in all the tasks that they imposed on them" (Exodus 1:13-14). Israelites were encouraged to "remember that you were a slave in the land of Egypt" and I (the Lord) redeemed you. Israel was a "slave in the land of Egypt" (Deuteronomy 5:15, 24:18, and 24:22). "[T]heir descendants who were still left in the land, whom the Israelites were unable to destroy completely — these

Solomon conscripted for slave labor, and so they are to this day" (1 Kings 9:21).

"When you buy a male Hebrew slave, he shall serve six years, but in the seventh he shall go out a free person, without debt" (Exodus 21:2). When sent out as a free person, the former owner must not send him out empty-handed. (See Deuteronomy 15:13.) Certain other rules followed. See Exodus 21:6-10.

Even Hebrew slaves were at the mercy of ruthless slave owners. Exodus 21:7 and 21:20-27 and Leviticus 19:20. While slaves had no power with tenants and sometimes suffered by them (see Luke 20:10), there were exceptions: When the centurion's highly valued slave was ill and close to death, the centurion sent Jewish elders to Jesus requesting him to come and heal his slave. (See Luke 7:2-3.)

Of the 100 references to "slave," fourteen occur in Matthew, four in Mark, and fifteen in Luke. Jesus directs attention to the relationship of slave or servant to the head of the household, so common that all could follow the metaphor: the slave forgiven his debt refuses to forgive a debt owed him (Matthew 18:23); the faithful and wise slave put in charge of the household is found at work by his returning master (Matthew 24:45-46); the trustworthy versus the wicked slave (Matthew 24:46ff and Luke 19:22); the faithful slave entrusted with much because he could be trusted with little (Matthew 25:21 and Luke 19:17); "No one can serve two masters; for a slave will either hate the one and love the other, or be devoted to the one and despise the other. You cannot serve God and wealth" (Matthew 6:24 and Luke 16:13); and "A disciple is not above the teacher, nor a slave above the master" (Matthew 10:24).

Three Pauline passages are worth noting. Paul merges physical slavery with obedience to Christ in a fashion that renders a deeper understanding of both types of service. Life in Christ transcends artificial divisions of "Jew or Greek ... slave or free ... male and female; for all of you are one in Christ Jesus" (Galatians 3:28).

Slaves, obey your earthly masters with fear and trembling, in singleness of heart, as you obey Christ; not only while being watched, and in order to please them,

but as slaves of Christ, doing the will of God from the
heart. Render service with enthusiasm, as to the Lord
and not to men and women, knowing that whatever good
we do, we will receive the same again from the Lord,
whether we are slaves or free.
*   And, masters, do the same to them. Stop threaten-*
ing them, for you know that both of you have the same
Master in heaven, and with him there is no partiality.
                                         — Ephesians 6:5-9

"Were you a slave when called? Do not be concerned about it. Even if you can gain your freedom, make use of your present condition now more than ever. For whoever was called in the Lord as a slave is a freed person belonging to the Lord, just as whoever was free when called is a slave of Christ" (1 Corinthian 7:21-22).

Worthless

"We are worthless slaves; we have only done what we ought to have done" (Luke 17:10b). God counters the worthlessness of a slave by elevating the concept of servant through the servanthood of Jesus. That which is worthless lacks value or is of no use, as throwaway as a paper towel. It is a term of depression: "All her people groan as they search for bread; they trade their treasures for food to revive their strength. Look, O Lord, and see how worthless I have become" (Lamentations 1:11).

"Worthless" appears in 33 other references. Among them are "worthless woman" (1 Samuel 1:16), "worthless and reckless fellows" (Judges 9:4 and 1 Samuel 10:27), "despised and worthless" (1 Samuel 15:9), "corrupt and worthless fellows" (1 Samuel 30:22), "worthless scoundrels" (2 Chronicles 13:7), "worthless physicians" (Job 13:4), "the worthless" (Psalm 26:4), "worthless idols" (Psalm 31:6 and 97:7), "human help is worthless" (Psalm 60:11 and 108:12), "a worthless witness" (Proverbs 19:28), "worthless pursuits" (Proverbs 28:19), "worthless and empty" (Isaiah 30:7), "worthless things" (Jeremiah 2:5 and 16:19), "worthless divination" (Jeremiah 14:14), "you are worthless" (Nahum 1:14), "worthless shepherd" (Zechariah 11:15 and 11:17), "worthless slave" (Matthew 25:30.)

202

4. Parallel Scripture

The parable of A Decent Obsession is special to Luke.

Mustard Seed

The writer addresses the disciples directly, using "you" three times: "The Lord replied, 'If *you* had faith the size of a mustard seed, *you* could say to this mulberry tree, "Be uprooted and planted in the sea," and it would obey *you'* " (Luke 17:6). Luke also speaks immediately of personal faith. Earlier, Luke is not as personal. He says "like a mustard seed that *someone* took." (See Luke 13:19.)

Matthew and Mark, as does Luke in the chapter 13 parallel, speak of the kingdom of heaven rather than personal faith. (See Matthew 13:31-32.) Making the "is like" analogy of the mustard seed, these writers keep the parable at a personal distance. They focus on the mustard seed, referring to "it" four times as they describe the seed and its growth into a tree that nesting birds see as welcome. (See Cycle A, Parable 4, The Parable Of The Sower and Cycle B, Parable 5, The Parable Of The Miracle Seed.)

Later, rather than the capacity of faith to move a mulberry tree, Matthew speaks of being able to move a mountain by command. Here, as does Luke in chapter 17, Matthew uses the personal, "you." (See Matthew 17:20.) This analogy is not in response to a request to be given faith. Rather, it answers the disciples' wondering why they had been unable to cure an epileptic. Jesus prefaces this response with "Because of our little faith" and speaks of the mustard seed/mountain. Matthew says that with this faith "nothing will be impossible for you" (Matthew 17:20b), while Luke steps back slightly from the personal and says, "and *it* would obey you" (Luke 17:6b).

At The Table

Compare " 'Come here at once and take your place at the table.' Would you not rather say to him, 'Prepare supper for me, put on your apron and serve me while I eat and drink; later you may eat and drink'?" (Luke 17:7b-8) with "For who is greater, the one who is at the table or the one who serves? Is it not the one at the table?

But I am among you as one who serves. You are those who have stood by me in my trials; and I confer on you, just as my Father has conferred on me, a kingdom, so that you may eat and drink at my table in my kingdom, and you will sit on thrones judging the twelve tribes of Israel" (Luke 22:27-30).

Again, compare with "It will not be so among you; but whoever wishes to be great among you must be your servant, and whoever wishes to be first among you must be your slave; just as the Son of Man came not to be served but to serve, and to give his life a ransom for many" (Matthew 20:26-28 and Mark 10:43-44).

5. Chat Room

Anthony: I suppose what frustrates me about this parable is also the very point Christ makes about increasing our faith. Become as "worthless slaves" who are just doing what they "ought to have done" without need for expression of gratitude or for advancement or elevation to the status of a freed person. Just let faith happen. It will take care of itself. A little faith carries far more than a dollop of impact.

Ramzi: So are you saying, be who you are and let your faith be what it is without making it a big deal? Your faith may seem as insignificant as a worthless slave, but look again. From God's viewpoint, you are beloved even if you were a supposedly worthless slave or even a servant. Christ submitted to a life of being a servant of God, a proclaimed beloved servant, at that.

Anthony: But a slave is at the bottom. I cringe at the thought of an enslavement. In Jesus' day, anyone could be made a slave, a political prisoner of sorts, at any moment, as a result of battle victories or in-house arrangements of servitude.

Ramzi: Fullness of life, fullness of being, a meaningful life, or however you want to say it is independent of temporal conditions of body, economics, or other circumstances that are beyond our control. Even a slave can transcend the involuntary enslavement to become a faithful and devoted servant.

Anthony: Are you sure?

Ramzi: As certain as I am that a sturdy, durable mulberry tree can emerge from its tiny seed.

Anthony: Well, yes, I get that, but I'm dubious about commanding the tree to uproot and plant itself in the sea.

Ramzi: Indeed. But then so might appear the tiniest thread of faith that somehow gathers to itself more fibers until it becomes a tightly woven, durable fabric.

Anthony: Or take my friend who was at first enslaved by a disability. It was so handicapping that his life seemed defined only by the disability. Then tenacity, perseverance, even stubbornness seeped in. He found new ways of accomplishing what was of greatest importance and transcended the disability to live the meaningful life of a whole person.

Maria: Faith that he could figure out the alternative route set him free. Oh, the discovered realm of freedom when constrained to live within a given limitation! Attitude, attitude, gratitude. Hi, I'm Maria. I just logged onto the chat room and want to add some thoughts.

Anthony: Welcome.

Maria: We do learn about serving from the Hebrews and early Christians. High quality people find themselves tossed into unexpected circumstances. Freedom is not the situation but how we respond to it and how we honor both ourselves and the one whom we serve.

Anthony: I find the "later" of most serving difficult. Serving takes time. In many daily relationships we must put ourselves last. That we all sit together at the Savior's table to receive the communion elements helps. We wait until everyone in the church, organist and worship leader included, holds the bread or juice. To me, partaking together erases differences and shapes an expression of respect. I remember Whose I am in spite of everything. Perhaps that is why such a tiny piece of bread and only a couple swallows of juice are so filling, so satisfying.

Ramzi: An attitude of service is not all that bad a way of relating to other people as long as we neither demean ourselves nor slip into thingification of those we serve. Whether physician or parent, schoolteacher or minister, airplane technician or a cook, clerk, or custodian, servanthood is honorable.

Maria: "Thingification," that is the exact feeling when you are served against your will as if you cannot do something for yourself.

Anthony: Or if you are told under duress to serve someone. Thingification is the opposite of our relationship to God and God's covenant with us.

Maria: The feeling tone of serving another reminds me of the journey of an assist dog from obedient response to devoted service above self. Devotion grows as surely as trust and as faith grow.

Ramzi: Where does devotion come from? Gratitude? How does faith grow? With service, the giving of one's self? With the discipline of service? When we know that we are free.

Parable 17

The Uncaring Judge

Luke 18:1-8

---

1. Text

Then Jesus told them a parable about their need to pray always and not to lose heart. [2] He said, "In a certain city there was a judge who neither feared God nor had respect for people. [3] In that city there was a widow who kept coming to him and saying, 'Grant me justice against my opponent.' [4] For a while he refused; but later he said to himself, 'Though I have no fear of God and no respect for anyone, [5] yet because this widow keeps bothering me, I will grant her justice, so that she may not wear me out by continually coming.' " [6] And the Lord said, "Listen to what the unjust judge says. [7] And will not God grant justice to his chosen ones who cry to him day and night? Will he delay long in helping them? [8] I tell you, he will quickly grant justice to them. And yet, when the Son of Man comes, will he find faith on earth?"

2. What's Happening?

First Point Of Action

Jesus tells the parable about our need to pray always and not lose heart.

Second Point Of Action

He describes the two characters, the judge who does not fear God or respect people and the widow who persists in coming to him to request justice against her opponent.

Third Point Of Action

The judge refuses for a while, then, to get rid of her, grants the woman justice.

Fourth Point Of Action

Jesus makes the analogy with our prayer relationship to God as one who grants justice without delay to those who persist with prayer.

Fifth Point Of Action

Jesus wonders, despite this, if the Son of Man will find such faith on earth.

3. Spadework

Chosen (Ones)

Those who are God's chosen, God calls by name: "... [A]nd Israel my chosen, I call you by your name, I surname you, though you do not know me" (Isaiah 45:4). The task of God's chosen ones is to clothe themselves "with compassion, kindness, humility, meekness, and patience" (Colossians 3:12). God's chosen "shall long enjoy the work of their hands" (Isaiah 65:22). God provides for them: "[F]or I give water in the wilderness, rivers in the desert, to give drink to my chosen people" (Isaiah 43:20).

Among the five other references to "chosen ones" are several Psalms. To God's chosen ones, God makes promises: "You said, 'I have made a covenant with my chosen one' ... 'I will establish your descendants forever, / and build your throne for all generations' " (Psalm 89:3-4). Joy and singing are the fruit of the struggle of God's chosen people: "So he brought his people out with joy, / his chosen ones with singing" (Psalm 105:43). See also Psalm 106:5. A whole body of people are God's chosen ones: "O offspring of his servant

Israel, children of Jacob, his chosen ones" (1 Chronicles 15:13). See also Psalm 105:6.

The "Servant" passage from Isaiah 42:1 is an invitation to consider how not only Christ but each person is God's chosen and called to open the way for bringing about God's justice, as did the Lukan widow: "Here is my servant, whom I uphold, my chosen, in whom my soul delights; I have put my spirit upon him; he will bring forth justice to the nations."

Cry To God

A cry is an earnest or urgent request, a plea. It is a prayer. Uttered loudly or called out, a lament is alive with the urgency of the unsummoned wail of one who keens with grief. Singing praise to God is easy and spontaneous. Jesus suggests that God would have the crying of our laments be as natural as our praising. We stall before admitting the necessity of making our complaint before God, ignoring that God already is aware of it. Either we are reluctant, or once we have begun to lament, we pour forth with the incessancy of a widow before an unjust judge. To whom else but our creator can we eventually submit the cry of the heart?

The pattern of the Psalmist, which includes both songs of praise and songs of lament, mirrors the existence of elation and desperation in the flow of human life. See especially Psalm 18:6, 28:2, and 57:2.

We cry out to God because first we trust that God has a design for our lives: "I cry to God Most High, / to God who fulfills his purpose for me" (Psalm 57:2). Without initial thought of answer, the Psalmist first hopes that God at least will hear. The Psalmist proceeds: "Hear the voice of my supplication, / as I cry to you for help, / as I lift up my hands / toward your most holy sanctuary" (Psalm 28:2). First, gain the attention of God: "Listen to the sound of my cry, / my King and my God, / for to you I pray" (Psalm 5:2).

When we cry out to God, we want some evidence that God hears. Job says, "I cry to you and you do not answer me; I stand, and you merely look at me" (Job 30:20). The sigh of relief at having been heard is clear in this Psalm: "In my distress I called upon the Lord; / to my God I cried for help. / From his temple he heard my voice, / and my cry to him reached his ears" (Psalm 18:6).

Do you approach God inviting the confidence of being heard? Do you call to God dominated by the fear of retribution for all your past shortcomings? The prophets, Micah and Habakkuk, suggest, "Then they will cry to the Lord, but he will not answer them; he will hide his face from them at that time, because they have acted wickedly," (Micah 3:4) and "O Lord, how long shall I cry for help, and you will not listen?" (Habakkuk 1:2a).

Christ answers uncertainty with the words of the present text: "And will not God grant justice to his chosen ones who cry to him day and night? Will he delay long in helping them? I tell you, he will quickly grant justice to them" (Luke 18:7-8a).

Justice/Unjust

While "justice" occurs biblically 121 times; "unjust" appears only thirteen times. One might be concerned about the capacity of an unjust judge to dispense justice. However, even the unjust judge in the present parable eventually takes the right action if for the wrong reason of getting rid of the persistent woman. Hebrew Scripture says this about giving an unjust judgment: "You shall not render an unjust judgment; you shall not be partial to the poor or defer to the great: with justice you shall judge your neighbor" (Leviticus 19:15).

While unjust judges abound, the judgment of God is trustworthy: "A faithful God, without deceit, just and upright is he" (Deuteronomy 32:4). "Of a truth, God will not do wickedly, and the Almighty will not pervert justice" (Job 34:12). "The Almighty — we cannot find him; he is great in power and justice, and abundant righteousness he will not violate" (Job 37:23).

In contrast to the unjust judge, God is a God of justice who acts justly. "[God] loves righteousness and justice; / the earth is full of the steadfast love of the Lord" (Psalm 33:5). See also Philippians 48.

God's judgments, as well as God's ways, are "just and true." (See Revelation 15:3 and 16:7.) "Therefore the Lord waits to be gracious to you; therefore he will rise up to show mercy to you. For the Lord is a God of justice; blessed are all those who wait for him" (Isaiah 30:18). "[B]ut let those who boast boast in this, that they understand and know me, that I am the Lord; I act with stead-fast love, justice, and righteousness in the earth, for in these things I delight, says the Lord" (Jeremiah 9:24).

God also expects the human family to act in a right way. "To do righteousness and justice is more acceptable to the Lord than sacrifice" (Proverbs 21:3). Among the other biblical charges to all regarding justice, including the unjust judge, are the following passages: "The mouths of the righteous utter wisdom, and their tongues speak justice" (Psalm 37:30). A just person is one of integrity. (See Job 31:6.) "May [your king] judge your people with righteousness, and your poor with justice" (Psalm 72:2).

"Give justice to the weak and the orphan; / maintain the right of the lowly and the destitute" (Psalm 82:3). "[L]earn to do good; seek justice, rescue the oppressed, defend the orphan, plead for the widow" (Isaiah 1:17). "Thus says the Lord: Act with justice and righteousness, and deliver from the hand of the oppressor anyone who has been robbed. And do no wrong or violence to the alien, the orphan, and the widow, or shed innocent blood in this place" (Jeremiah 22:3). See also the justice standards of Micah 6:8 and Amos 5:15 and 5:24.

Who appears chosen as God's servant is at times a surprise. In this parable, the widow is servant: "Here is my servant, whom I uphold, my chosen, in whom my soul delights; I have put my spirit upon him; he will bring forth justice to the nations" (Isaiah 42:1).

Consider the perseverence of the praying widow also from the perspective of these passages: "[A] bruised reed he will not break, and a dimly burning wick he will not quench; he will faithfully bring forth justice. He will not grow faint or be crushed until he has established justice in the earth; and the coastlands wait for his teaching" (Isaiah 42:3-4).

The widow's insistence reflects an innate understanding of the God of these passages: "The evil do not understand justice, but those who seek the Lord understand it completely" (Proverbs 28:5). "But as for you, return to your God, hold fast to love and justice, and wait continually for your God" (Hosea 12:6).

Lose (Lost) Heart

This phrase occurs a dozen times in the Bible. Warriors in the stories of Hebrew Scripture know about losing heart during strife. (See Genesis 42:28, 2 Samuel 22:46, and Psalm 18:45.) Those who "lose heart" may be afraid, panic, or dread. They may withdraw. (See Deuteronomy 20:3 and Daniel 11:30.)

In addition to the present text, which is the only instance in the Gospels, six other usages of "lose heart" occur in the New Testament. Two references, reflecting an understanding of the tenderheartedness of children, speak to the child-parent relationships. (See Colossians 3:21 and Hebrews 12:5.) When the struggles of early Christianity threatened to dishearten the churches of Paul's day, the writers of the letters spoke about losing heart. (See 2 Corinthians 4:1, Ephesians 3:13, and Hebrews 12:3.)

Among the most memorable of the exhortations not to "lose heart" is that from 2 Corinthians 4:16-18: "So we do not lose heart. Even though our outer nature is wasting away, our inner nature is being renewed day by day. For this slight momentary affliction is preparing us for an eternal weight of glory beyond all measure, because we look not at what can be seen but at what cannot be seen; for what can be seen is temporary, but what cannot be seen is eternal."

Prayer

Of the three parables about prayer in this cycle, "The Midnight Friend" (Cycle C, Parable 7) speaks to the God and pray-er relationship as one of faithfulness and persistence. The present parable focuses on persistence and the encouragement of praying, whereas The Two Men At Prayer (Cycle C, Parable 18) emphasizes attitude when praying.

As a sign of unceasing persistence, the "day and night" phrase appears on 27 occasions from Genesis 8:22 to Revelation 20:10. The prophet Nehemiah spoke of persistent prayer, "... I now pray before you day and night for your servants, the people of Israel, confessing the sins of the people of Israel, which we have sinned against you ..." (Nehemiah 1:6).

212

Others also speak of meditating "day and night" (Joshua 1:8 and Psalm 1:2), pleading before God day and night (1 Kings 8:59), keeping one's eyes open toward the house of God day and night (2 Chronicles 6:20), weeping day and night (Psalm 42:3, Lamentations 2:18, and Jeremiah 9:1), worshiping day and night (Acts 26:7 and Revelation 7:15), singing day and night (Revelation 6:8), and tormented day and night (Revelation 20:10). In thirteen other instances of persistence, the praying, working, howling, and crying went on "night and day."

Job asks everyone's questions. What good is prayer, anyway? One moment Job asks, "What is the Almighty, that we should serve him? And what profit do we get if we pray to him?" (Job 21:15). Next he asserts, "You will pray to him, and he will hear you" (Job 22:27). The subsequent question is implicit in Jeremiah's response to the commanders of the forces who asked that he pray for them, that is: Are you ready to hear the answer? Jeremiah told to all, "Very well: I am going to pray to the Lord your God as you request, and whatever the Lord answers you I will tell you; I will keep nothing back from you" (Jeremiah 42:4).

Jesus prayed. He trusted prayer. He recommended prayer, at a serious time, albeit with a pinch of sarcasm, to the disciples who had fallen asleep while Jesus prayed at Gethsemane: "[A]nd he said to them, 'Why are you sleeping? Get up and pray that you may not come into the time of trial' " (Luke 22:46).

4. Parallel Scripture

The parable, The Uncaring Judge, is special to Luke. However, the following passages are worth noting:

"Rejoice always, *pray without ceasing,* give thanks in all circumstances; for this is the will of God in Christ Jesus for you" (1 Thessalonians 5:16-18);

"You have *wearied the Lord with your words.* Yet you say, 'How have we wearied him?' By saying, 'All who do evil are good in the sight of the Lord, and he delights in them.' Or by asking, 'Where is the God of justice?' " (Malachi 2:17);

"The *prayer of the righteous is powerful and effective*" (James 5:16b);

"You must not be partial in judging: *hear out the small and the great alike*; you shall not be intimidated by anyone, for the judgment is God's" (Deuteronomy 1:17a);

"For the Lord loves justice; / *he will not forsake his faithful ones*" (Psalm 37:28); and

> For God is not unjust; he will not overlook your work and the love that you showed for his sake in serving the saints, as you still do. And we want each one of you to show the same diligence so as to realize the full assurance of hope to the very end, so that you may not become sluggish, but imitators of those who through faith and patience inherit the promises.
> — Hebrews 6:10-12

5. Chat Room

Adam: Most of the justice that happens around here is the result of stubborn persistence. The desire for change may be the goal of many people, but only a few have the tenacity to pursue that change lifelong, if necessary. Judges, by definition, are supposed to be just. Justice is supposed to happen. "Supposed to" has its gaps.

Brenda: The widow of Jesus' day had no clout. She was already in the cellar of society. However, this woman's position does not deter her. Lady, you must be some woman to persevere before the judge.

Deborah: And I supposed that I had no clout as a widow. If a filibuster of prayer — and that is what keeps me coming again and again and again — if a filibuster of prayer will wear down that crooked judge, then I have time.

Brenda: What keeps you from losing heart, Deborah, persisting day and night like that?

Deborah: Being on the side of what is right gives me energy. My God is some God. That is what being fed up with injustice finally does. You take on the corporation even if it costs your job. You refuse to move to the back of the bus. You just one day do what you need to do, almost without a plan, even though your skin is all that holds together the jelly of your viscera. You boycott your own church because your neighbor cannot get her wheelchair through the door. You cannot wait longer for someone else to make the changes. You become a Rosa Parks, and that is that.

Brenda: Is that what it takes to untie the political knots and unite the human family? Harangue "the judges" into right action with a quiet voice or with a noisy sound until they realize you will not go away. Your argument is sound, and they know, that you know, that they know it.

Adam: Our Middle Eastern brothers and sisters have owned that persistence. Was it a loss of heart that stopped their talking and started the pouring of concrete? I wonder if justice will ever happen. Why does the ancient prayer not work?

Deborah: We cannot give up. Our struggle is centuries old. We must not give in to terror now. God is on the side of justice.

Brenda: Your brokenheartedness has turned your prayer into the building of the wall. Adam, to what ancient prayer were you referring?

Adam: The Psalm Jewish folk have been praying for generations of mothers and fathers and children: "Pray for the peace of Jerusalem: / 'May they prosper who love you. / Peace be within your walls, / and security within your towers.' / For the sake of my relatives and friends I will say, 'Peace be within you' " (Psalm 122:7-8). Where is this "shalom" that these two peoples share with two different pronunciations? Will this prayer ever find an answer?

Deborah: Is it through incessant prayer that our physical barrier, this 215-mile wall, is being constructed lest no one will be left to argue? Sometimes justice takes unexpected forms. It is through the hope that faithfulness to prayer brings, however, that this time-out-for-survival-wall eventually will come down.

Can we possibly empower the knocked down wall between the former East Berlin and West Berlin to buoy our hope also? We are people. We are trying to cook the evening meal. We are trying to raise families. Our children are hoping to complete school.

Adam: When I think my capacity to make a positive difference in the world's areas of chaos and uncertainty is negligible, then I am looking at too large a perspective. I need to reduce the scale. I need to zoom in until my focus can perceive where I can make a constructive impact. Sometimes that focus is one on one. Sometimes it is an entire community.

Brenda: Person to person is the beginning point of injustice. It is also the beginning point of justice.

Deborah: For me, God is the beginning point of hope. Yet, hope needs a human vehicle.

Adam: Justice only happens with the right actions of chosen members of the human family. Okay, I must ask: Who is chosen, and who is not? Dare we include ourselves among God's chosen to receive God's justice? Dare we recognize that we might have been chosen to ascertain that God's justice happens within the realm of God?

Deborah: I can speak only for myself. I would never have volunteered to stand up to the judge. From deep within my soul, I had to do it. That is how God let me know that I am God's chosen one for this particular task. It was a dawning as powerful as my earlier realization that I am a chosen recipient of God's love and justice. That is the birth of faith.

Brenda: I've been thinking about that wall that cuts off your land from friendship. A wall of words may as well be a two-story high concrete wall when the heart is incapable of listening. Does prayer actually help to bring down walls, or is prayer wishful thinking? Where does prayer come in here? What does prayer do to the prayer? How does it connect with the one for whom the prayer is offered?

Deborah: Prayer is that sorting out of our thoughts that keeps us focused and strengthens our hearts. Prayer cleans out the debilitating debris of dismay that builds up through daily conflict. Our crying out day and night is not always with words. It is our openness to God's presence. Prayer helps me to avoid being overcome by impossibility.

Brenda: God's response is immediate. The world's justice requires human time.

Adam: This chat room exchange takes me back to Jesus' "And yet."

Brenda: Christ's "And yet?"

Adam: Yes. At the conclusion of the parable of The Unjust Judge, after Jesus assures us that God does not take forever to bring justice, Jesus says, "And yet, when the Son of Man comes, will he find faith on earth?"

Deborah: That statement of frustration with the human condition reveals to me the depth of Jesus' compassion. While offering you assurance, he knows firsthand how difficult it is to maintain hope.

Brenda: Christ appreciates the effort required to keep faith in possibility. He knows about reducing the gap between the reality of the human condition and God's hope for us.

217

Parable 18

Two Men At Prayer

Luke 18:9-14

---

1. Text

[Jesus] also told this parable to some who trusted in themselves that they were righteous and regarded others with contempt: [10] "Two men went up to the temple to pray, one a Pharisee and the other a tax collector. [11] The Pharisee, standing by himself, was praying thus, 'God, I thank you that I am not like other people: thieves, rogues, adulterers, or even like this tax collector. [12] I fast twice a week; I give a tenth of all my income.'[13] But the tax collector, standing far off, would not even look up to heaven, but was beating his breast and saying, 'God, be merciful to me, a sinner!' [14] I tell you, this man went down to his home justified rather than the other; for all who exalt themselves will be humbled, but all who humble themselves will be exalted."

2. What's Happening?

First Point Of Action

Jesus compares the self-righteous Pharisee with the humble person, a tax collector.

Second Point Of Action

The Pharisee self-praises to God as one who is better than others. The Pharisee lists attributes according to the letter of the Law credentials.

Third Point Of Action

Too humble to look toward heaven as he prayed, the tax collector berated himself through the beating of his breast and the words of his prayer.

Fourth Point Of Action

Jesus comments on humility versus self-glorification.

3. Spadework

Fast

When properly observed, fasting is an act of humbling the soul before God: "When I humbled my soul / with fasting, / they insulted me for doing / so" (Psalm 69:10). Again in Hebrew Scripture, fasting is a God-directed act:

> *Then his servants said to [David when his child by Uriah died], "What is this thing that you have done? You fasted and wept for the child while it was alive; but when the child died, you rose and ate food." He said, "While the child was still alive, I fasted and wept; for I said, 'Who knows? The Lord may be gracious to me, and the child may live.' But now he is dead; why should I fast? Can I bring him back again? I shall go to him, but he will not return to me."* — 2 Samuel 12:21-23

Of the eleven biblical references to "fasted," only the following occurs in the New Testament:

> *Then Jesus was led up by the Spirit into the wilderness to be tempted by the devil. He fasted forty days and forty nights, and afterwards he was famished. The tempter came and said to him, "If you are the Son of God, command these stones to become loaves of bread." But he answered, "It is written, 'One does not live by bread alone, but by every word that comes from the mouth of God.'"* — Matthew 4:1-4

Of those usages of "fast" as the withholding of food, fifteen occur in Hebrew Scripture. "Fasting" appears eleven times in Hebrew Scripture. Five of the six New testament references to "fast" appear in the Synoptic Gospels. Four of six New Testament references to "fasting" refer to the above verses in the Gospels of Luke, Mark, and Matthew.

Christ redirects the act of fasting to God rather than as the ostentatious activity displayed by Pharisees:

> *And whenever you fast, do not look dismal, like the hypocrites, for they disfigure their faces so as to show others that they are fasting. Truly I tell you, they have received their reward. But when you fast, put oil on your head and wash your face, so that your fasting may be seen not by others but by your Father who is in secret; and your Father who sees in secret will reward you.*
> — Matthew 6:16-18

Again, Jesus' focus is on a meaningful fast rather than a frequent but empty ritual done for the wrong reason:

> *Then they said to him, "John's disciples, like the disciples of the Pharisees, frequently fast and pray, but your disciples eat and drink." Jesus said to them, "You cannot make wedding guests fast while the bridegroom is with them, can you? The days will come when the bridegroom will be taken away from them, and then they will fast in those days."* — Luke 5:33-35
> (See also Matthew 9:14ff and Mark 2:18ff.)

For an eloquent explanation of fasting as a means of promoting justice and social change, see Isaiah 58:3-9:

> *"Why do we fast, but you do not see? Why humble ourselves, but you do not notice?" Look, you serve your own interest on your fast day, and oppress all your workers. Look, you fast only to quarrel and to fight and to strike with a wicked fist. Such fasting as you do*

today will not make your voice heard on high. Is such the fast that I choose, a day to humble oneself? Is it to bow down the head like a bulrush, and to lie in sackcloth and ashes?

Will you call this a fast, a day acceptable to the Lord? Is not this the fast that I choose: to loose the bonds of injustice, to undo the thongs of the yoke, to let the oppressed go free, and to break every yoke? Is it not to share your bread with the hungry, and bring the homeless poor into your house; when you see the naked, to cover them, and not to hide yourself from your own kin?

Then your light shall break forth like the dawn, and your healing shall spring up quickly; your vindicator shall go before you, the glory of the Lord shall be your rear guard. Then you shall call, and the Lord will answer; you shall cry for help, and he will say, Here I am.

In further contrast to the sober-faced but false fasting of the Pharisee, the prophet Zechariah proclaims that some of the fasts, "shall be seasons of joy and gladness, and cheerful festivals for the house of Judah: therefore love truth and peace" (Zechariah 8:19).

Humble

Twice, Christ refers to himself as humble: "Take my yoke upon you, and learn from me; for I am gentle and *humble* in heart, and you will find rest for your souls" (Matthew 11:29). See also Matthew 21:5, the Palm Sunday entry to Jerusalem.

Humility is a difficult concept. It has little to do with prideful or arrogant behavior but rather deprives an individual of self-esteem or self-worth. It suggests a modesty and purity both of spirit and behavior. One who is humble is unpretentious, lacking a sense of self-importance. To be humble is not to be humiliated, which is a suffering of loss of self-respect or dignity. The usual synonyms for humble may appear unappetizing to a well-balanced Christian of today who also is in prime mental and spiritual health.

"Humble" occurs 38 times in the Bible, 26 of which are found in the Hebrew Scripture. Of the dozen references in the New Testament, six appear in the Gospels of Matthew and Luke. (See Section 4 of this chapter.)

Christ had a predecessor whom God lifted up because of his humility. "Now the man Moses was very humble, more so than anyone else on the face of the earth" (Numbers 12:3). Because of Moses' humility, God defended Moses when Miriam and Aaron decried his marriage to a Cushite woman. God said that when prophets were around, he spoke to them in visions and dreams. However, God entrusts Moses with all his house: "With him I speak face to face — clearly, not in riddles; and he beholds the form of the Lord" (Numbers 12:8).

Humility gains status with God. Humility, along with praying, seeking God's face, and turning from wicked ways, is requisite to God's hearing, forgiving, and healing. (See 2 Chronicles 7:14.) In contrast to the disgrace that comes with pride, wisdom accompanies those who are humble. (See Proverbs 11:2.)

God takes an active role in the life of the humble. "[God] leads the humble in what is right, and teaches the humble his way" (Psalm 25:9). God "revive[s] the spirit of the humble, and revive[s] the heart of the contrite" (Isaiah 57:15). See also Isaiah 66:2.

The author of 1 Peter sums up the way of the Christian: "Finally, all of you, have unity of spirit, sympathy, love for one another, a tender heart, and a humble mind" (1 Peter 3:8).

Pharisee(s)

Were advocates of the Kohlberg (Piaget) theory of progressive moral/religious growth to characterize the developmental level of the Pharisees, they might perceive them as stuck at the people-pleasing law and order stage that hinges on responding to duty.[1] The Pharisees condemn Jesus for eating with or even associating with sinners and tax collectors. (See Mark 2:16, Luke 5:30, and Luke 7:39.) The Pharisees notice that Jesus does not follow the traditional ritual of hand washing before dinner. (See Luke 11:37-38.)

By contrast, Jesus criticizes the Pharisees for seeing no farther than obedience to the letter of the law. According to Jesus, the Pharisaic understanding of the law is backward. They neglect the important human and humanizing dimensions of justice, mercy, and faith but are good at tithing mint, dill, and cummin. (See Matthew 23:23.)

Jesus chides the hypocritical ways of the Pharisees that cannot envision human possibility: "But woe to you, scribes and Pharisees, hypocrites! For you lock people out of the kingdom of heaven. For you do not go in yourselves, and when others are going in, you stop them" (Matthew 23:13), and "You blind Pharisee! First clean the inside of the cup, so that the outside also may become clean" (Matthew 23:26).

Christ's task was to draw the human family toward a higher level of existence. He himself attained the apex of moral thinking, the level of "principled conscience."[2] At this level of moral awareness, one practices a genuine interest in the welfare of others, respecting universal principles and the demands of individual conscience.

Nine biblical references to "Pharisee" and 79 references to "Pharisees" appear in the New Testament. In addition to two named men, Nicodemus and Gamaliel, identified biblically as Pharisees (John 3:1 and Acts 5:34), the Apostle Paul identified himself as a Pharisee. His testimony to King Agrippa II offers further understanding to this sect. Paul testified before the king that he once "belonged to the strictest sect of our religion and lived as a Pharisee" (Acts 26:5). Before the council, he said, "Brothers, I am a Pharisee, a son of Pharisees. I am on trial concerning the hope of the resurrection of the dead" (Acts 23:6).

In the letter to the Philippians, he gave the following description of his earlier lifestyle and his renunciation of that way of life:

> ... *[C]ircumcised on the eighth day, a member of the people of Israel, of the tribe of Benjamin, a Hebrew born of Hebrews;* as to the law, a Pharisee; *as to zeal, a persecutor of the church;* as to righteousness under the law, blameless ... *For his sake I have suffered the loss*

of all things, and I regard them as rubbish, *in order that I may gain Christ and be found in him,* not having a righteousness of my own that comes from the law, but one that comes through faith in Christ, the righteousness from God based on faith.   — Philippians 3:5-9

Pray(er)

See Cycle C, Parable 7, A Midnight Friend and Cycle C, Parable 17, The Uncaring Judge.

Righteous

Of the 217 references to "righteous," 165 occur in the Hebrew Scripture. The Psalms contain 56 references with 51 in Proverbs. In the New Testament, 22 of the 52 usages appear in the Gospels. "Righteousness" appears 194 times.

In Genesis, Noah is described as a righteous person, that is, "blameless in his generation" (Genesis 6:9). The righteous are not wicked. (See Genesis 18:25.) Saul said David was more righteous then he, "for you have repaid me good, whereas I have repaid you evil" (1 Samuel 24:17).

"Bold as a lion," the righteous fulfill their promises, do what is lawful and right, offer good advice to friends, hate falsehood, ponder their answers, and find refuge in their integrity. (See Nehemiah 9:8, Ezekiel 18:5, Proverbs 12:26, 13:5, 14:32, 15:28, and 28:1.) "[T]here is nothing twisted or crooked in" the words of the righteous (Proverbs 8:8). "The fruit of the righteous is a tree of life" (Proverbs 11:30). "[T]he righteous give and do not hold back" (Proverbs 21:26). The righteous know the rights of the poor. (See Proverbs 29:6.)

Both Eliphaz and Bildad wonder aloud, "Can mortals be righteous before God? Can human beings be pure before their Maker?" (Job 4:17). See also Job 25:4. Even as he ponders, Job concludes, "Yet the righteous hold to their way, and they that have clean hands grow stronger and stronger" (Job 17:9). The righteous one serves God. (See Malachi 3:18.)

The Psalmist speaks often of righteousness. The righteous are upright in heart and are joyful. (See Psalm 11:7, 32:11, and 68:3.)

"The mouths of the righteous utter wisdom, and their tongues speak justice" (Psalm 37:30). See also Psalm 94:15. The righteous leave judging to God: "Surely there is a reward for the righteous; surely there is a God who judges on earth" (Psalm 58:11). "Better is a little that the righteous person has than the abundance of many wicked" (Psalm 37:16).

On the down side, the philosopher writes, "In my vain life I have seen everything; there are righteous people who perish in their righteousness, and there are wicked people who prolong their life in their evildoing" (Ecclesiastes 7:15).

Jesus lambasts the *self-righteous* Pharisees as hypocrites who present themselves as righteous. In addition to the present text: "Woe to you, scribes and Pharisees, hypocrites! For you are like whitewashed tombs, which on the outside look beautiful, but inside they are full of the bones of the dead and of all kinds of filth" (Matthew 23:27). In addition to today's text, see Luke 5:32.

Christ realizes the gap between reality and the ideal. He understands human nature and has compassion for the imperfect person who is trying to do better: "Go and learn what this means, 'I desire mercy, not sacrifice.' For I have come to call not the righteous but sinners" (Matthew 9:13); "When Jesus heard this, he said to them, 'Those who are well have no need of a physician, but those who are sick; I have come to call not the righteous but sinners' " (Mark 2:17); and "Just so, I tell you, there will be more joy in heaven over one sinner who repents than over ninety-nine righteous persons who need no repentance" (Luke 15:7).

Christ presents a God great and merciful enough to encompass both the unrighteous and those who are trying to live right: "But I say to you, Love your enemies and pray for those who persecute you, so that you may be children of your Father in heaven; for he makes his sun rise on the evil and on the good, and sends rain on the righteous and on the unrighteous" (Matthew 5:44-45).

Tax Collector

While the Pharisees ostracized tax collectors, Christ's attitude toward them was that of inclusion. See the story about Zacchaeus in Luke 9:12ff. See also the story about Levi in Luke 5:27 and the calling of Matthew in Matthew 10:3. Zacchaeus, Levi, and Matthew were tax collectors. See also Cycle C, Parable 4, The Prodigal Sons.

Tithe(s)

Twelve biblical references cite "tithes" and thirteen use "tithe." Eleven are located in the Pentateuch. The first instance of tithing occurs in the first book of the Law: "And Abram gave [the king of Sodom] one tenth of everything" (Genesis 14:20b). The next occurrence relates to Jacob's promise after his ladder dream: "Then Jacob made a vow, a gift of gratitude, saying, 'If God will be with me, and will keep me in this way that I go, and will give me bread to eat and clothing to wear, so that I come again to my father's house in peace, then the Lord shall be my God ... and of all that you give me I will surely give one tenth to you' " (Genesis 28:20-22).

The tithe then was a gift for the support of the priests and the religious leaders, the tribe of Levi who were entrusted with the tabernacle, in return for the service they performed. They had no allotment in their land and were to set apart a tithe of the tithe. See Numbers 18:20-21 and 18:25-27. See also Deuteronomy 14:22-23, and 28-29, and 26:12; 2 Chronicles 31:4-6; Nehemiah 10:38 and 13:12; and Malachi 3:10.

The two New Testament references to tithing by Jesus are of a critical nature. With woe, Jesus singles out the hypocritical scribes and Pharisees: "But woe to you Pharisees! For you tithe mint and rue and herbs of all kinds, and neglect justice and the love of God; it is these you ought to have practiced, without neglecting the others" (Luke 11:42). See also Matthew 23:23.

4. Parallel Scripture

The present text reads, "I tell you, this man went down to his home justified rather than the other; for all who exalt themselves will be humbled, *but all* who humble themselves will be exalted" (Luke 18:14b). In the parable of the Wedding Banquet, Jesus said, "For all who exalt themselves will be humbled, *and those* who

227

humble themselves will be exalted" (Luke 14:11). (See Cycle A, Parable 11, Places Of Honor.)

Speaking to the crowds and to his disciples about the Pharisees, Jesus said, "All who exalt themselves will be humbled, *and all* who humble themselves will be exalted" (Matthew 23:12). See also Matthew 18:4: "Whoever *becomes humble* like this child is the greatest in the kingdom of heaven."

5. Chat Room

Newer Christian: I must admit to getting a chuckle out of the "gray hair" Proverb. Do you remember it? "Gray hair is a crown of glory; it is gained in a righteous life" (Proverbs 16:31). Now that makes one think twice about being righteous! To me it is a puzzle. My goal is to be righteous, yet if I think I approach being righteous, I probably am self-righteous. I have no desire to effuse pride. I would like to be seen as humble, yet I feel great after doing something meaningful for others.

Seasoned Christian: Seems to me you are rather hard on yourself. Persistence, not perfection, is the goal here. When we stumble, we rise and continue to try moving forward. For me, being righteous and being humble are something like being courageous.

A friend once confided that others said to her, "With all your disabilities, you are such a courageous person." The friend thought courage must be one of those qualities others see in you. It must be reflected because she did not feel courageous. She simply arose each day and kept plugging along. Bit by bit, not realizing how others perceived her, she moved forward through her day and her career.

Newer Christian: I want being a Christian to make a difference in my life. How do I let others know that I am a Christian? It is more than a cross around my neck or God-talk or carrying a Bible. That would embarrass me. I take my faith seriously, but I do not want to be dubbed a goodie-goodie.

228

Seasoned Christian: There is a time for wearing a cross and using God-talk and carrying a Bible. My guess is you could be doing all that with the attitude of showing others you are a practicing Christian and they still would say, "You're no real Christian."

Newer Christian: If one suggested, for instance, that a couple were to enter church wearing unsuitable clothing, I would still welcome them and disregard their appearance, lifestyle, or any other differences that might set them apart.

Seasoned Christian: And if you met the same folks in town on a cold day, you might cross the street to offer a couple jackets rather than scorn. The way we treat others tells more about the influence of Christ upon our lives than the external trappings of our religion.

Newer Christian: What about tithing? Is sharing ten percent of my income enough?

Seasoned Christian: Is it more than you can afford? Is it within your means? Those are the questions to consider first.

Newer Christian: I feel guilty when the volunteers for cancer and diabetes and heart and arthritis all come around. I give what I can. It adds up. I find enough to share. To volunteer to acquire $100 worth of pledges or walk five miles for CROP works better for me.

Seasoned Christian: There are many ways to share in addition to giving part of your money. The giving of your time, your compassion, and your talents also reflects a generous heart. The spirit of your giving makes the difference. That is the new law about giving beyond the external decrees that might be perfunctory or for show.

Newer Christian: If giving of myself and being a welcoming person are dimensions of righteousness in the best sense, then my alertness to the needs and cares of others and to how I might respond are valuable.

Also A Christian: Hello. I have been following your exchange on my office screen. I am a wealthy woman with money to share. As a result, others approach me constantly. I give to my church as part of my membership responsibility. However, I feel that my real giving is the quiet gift. Through the years, I have sent our church's children to camp, assumed budget shortfalls for seniors, and helped with college tuition.

Newer Christian: Hello to you. I agree that it is okay to feel pleased about what you do.

Also A Christian: That is how I feel about it. I neither berate myself for not giving more nor do I broadcast what I do. It is enough that God is aware. My heart is thankful for the means to be generous.

Seasoned Christian: I like to focus upon the positive energy of our faith. A negative stance of extreme self-denial or humility that approaches self-humiliation can only be excessive. Respect for the whole human family includes respecting ourselves.

Newer Christian: Righteousness is about the justice of being a fully welcoming person. It comes from the inside. Can we ever trust in ourselves that we are the humble righteous?

Seasoned Christian: Only God can judge that.

Also A Christian: I believe a piece of God lives within us that recognizes the right way to live.

Also A Christian: When we begin to understand Christ's view of the righteous and the unrighteous, we begin to understand humility. There is no room for artificial behavior adopted to impress others.

New Christian: Then how we pray mirrors how we live as Christians.

Also A Christian: And how we live reflects how we pray.

---

1. Robert N. Barger. "A Summary Of Lawrence Kohlberg's Stages of Moral De-velopment," copyright 2000 by Robert N. Barger, Ph.D. University of Notre Dame Notre Dame, Indiana 46556. Http://www.nd.edu/~rbarger/kohlberg.html.

2. *Ibid.*

Word Study Index

233

Bibliography

Barger, Robert N., "A Summary of Lawrence Kohlberg's Stages of Moral Development" (Notre Dame, Indiana: University of Notre Dame, 2001), on http://www.nd.edu/!rbarger/kkohlber.html.

Benson, Herbert, *The Relaxation Response* (New York: Morrow, William and Company, 2000).

Brauninger, Dallas A., *Holy E-Mail* (Lima, Ohio: CSS Publishing Co., Inc., 2001).

_____, *Preaching the Miracles* (Lima, Ohio: CSS Publishing Co., Inc., 1988), Series II, Cycle A.

Bultmann, Rudolf, *Jesus and the Word* (Full text on www.religion-online.org prepared for Religion Online by Ted and Winnie Brock using [New York: Charles Scribner's Sons, 1958]).

Buttrick, George A., *The Interpreter's Dictionary of the Bible* (Nashville: Abingdon Press, 1962), 4 volumes.

Eiesland, Nancy L., *The Disabled God: Toward a Liberatory Theology* (Nashville: Abingdon Press, 1994).

McFague, Sallie, *Speaking in Parables: A Study in Metaphor and Theology* (Full text on www.religion-online.org prepared for Religion Online by Dick and Sue Kendall using [Philadelphia: Fortress Press, 1975]).

Niebuhr, Reinhold, *The Nature and Destiny of Man: A Christian Interpretation* (New York: Charles Scribner's Sons, 1964), volumes 1 and 2.

Perrin, Norman, *Jesus and the Language of the Kingdom: Symbol and Metaphor in New Testament Interpretation* (Philadelphia: Fortress Press, 1976).

Spektor, Alex, "September 11 Victims" [Text on www.september11victims.com] (c. 2001-2002).

Tillich, Paul, *Systematic Theology* (Chicago: University of Chicago Press, 1963), volume 3.

Via, Dan Otto, *The Parables, Their Literary and Existential Dimension* (Philadelphia: Fortress Press, 1967).

Whitehead, Alfred North, *Process and Reality* (New York: Harper and Row, 1960).